CENTENNIAL STATE TROLLEYS

By Ken Fletcher

(FRONT COVER)
This acrylic painting of Denver Tramway car 117 and trailer 616 was created by Denver native Joe Priselac. The cars are westbound on the original 16th Street Viaduct, with the tower of Union Station appearing on the left. The viaduct was built in 1889 for use by cable cars and later was used by electric streetcars. It was replaced in 1924 with a new structure that accommodated both transit and private vehicles. Streetcars last crossed the viaduct in July 1950. In January 1994, demolition began on the existing structure. There will be no replacement for it.

(BACK COVER)
It is October 26, 1947 and in one month trolleys would vanish from the streets of Pueblo. Car 126 crosses Union Avenue Bridge on its way to Minnequa Park. Most structures in the background are now part of the Union Avenue Historic District. *(R.H. Kindig photo)*

The Colorado Railroad Museum was established in 1958 to gather and preserve a tangible historical record of Colorado's fascinating railroad era. The Museum's invaluable collection of records, artifacts and equipment was begun in 1949, and the accumulation of important material is still continuing. The Museum is now operated by the not-for-profit Colorado Railroad Historical Foundation, Inc., in which your support and participation are cordially invited.

Centennial State Trolleys

hardcover ISBN 0-918654-52-1
softcover ISBN 0-918654-51-3
Library of Congress Catalog Card No. 95-069935

Printed and bound in the United States of America by Johnson Printing Company, Boulder, Colorado. Layout and design by Ken Fletcher, production by Richard A. Cooley.

PRINTED ON ACID FREE PAPER

Photographed in 1919, Denver Tramway motorman Ed Kelly hams it up for the photographer. *(Gene McKeever collection)*

CONTENTS

Acknowledgments 4
Colorado Map 5
Introduction 6–10

ASPEN 11
BOULDER 13
COLORADO SPRINGS 21
CRIPPLE CREEK DISTRICT 31
DENVER 37
DENVER & INTERURBAN 91
DURANGO 97
ENGLEWOOD 101
FORT COLLINS 103
GRAND JUNCTION 111
GREELEY 117
LEADVILLE 121
LITTLETON 123
MANITOU SPRINGS 127
MARBLE 131
PUEBLO 133
TRINIDAD 153
PAPER TIGERS 159

Bibliography 160

DEDICATION

This book is dedicated, with utmost appreciation, to the following gentlemen: W. Morris Cafky, Ed Haley, Dick Kindig, Gene McKeever and Don Robertson. You hold in your hands the product of their kind consideration, fine collections and vast knowledge of the subject.

ACKNOWLEDGMENTS

Any person who feels an urge to publish discovers quickly that many people must be relied upon and become involved, out of necessity, to assist in making the idea become a reality. Those are the folks who make the job of the author much easier and consequently save him untold hours that would otherwise have to be spent on frustrating and fruitless hunting expeditions.

I am indebted to Joe Priselac, for allowing the use of his excellent painting that graces the cover of this book; Barbara Foley and Rebecca Lintz at the Colorado Historical Society, who went above and beyond the call of duty in searching out some of the rare photographs that appear on these pages; Judge Dean C. Mabry, for the informative and entertaining tour amongst the remnants of the Trinidad system; Bill Penny of Denver, who loaded up a great part of his library and physically brought it to me for my perusal while searching for some minute fact or figure; Bruce Hanson, Mary Ruhland and Kathey Swan of the Western History Department of the Denver Public Library, who accommodated my every whim when searching through the vast collection of photographs in their department; Syd Joseph of Aurora, for providing samples from his extensive collection of transit tokens; John W. Maxwell of Wheat Ridge, who on short notice came up with some first-rate photos of Pueblo; Roger Smith of Fort Collins, for supplying a photo by the late Al Kilminster; Jody Corruccini at the Carnegie Branch Library for Local History in Boulder, for her gracious assistance in locating some heretofore unpublished photos of the Denver & Interurban and the local system in Boulder; Noreen Riffe at the Pueblo Library, for her amiable assistance; Rick Valdez, senior planner for the Pueblo Bus System, for allowing the use of a remarkable picture of an ersatz Birney; Jim Bewley at the Pueblo City Engineering Office, for providing useful 1922 track maps of Pueblo; Chip Sherman for responding to an eleventh-hour request for the color photo of Fort Collins and last but by no means least Darrell Arndt, for the use of his superb color night shot.

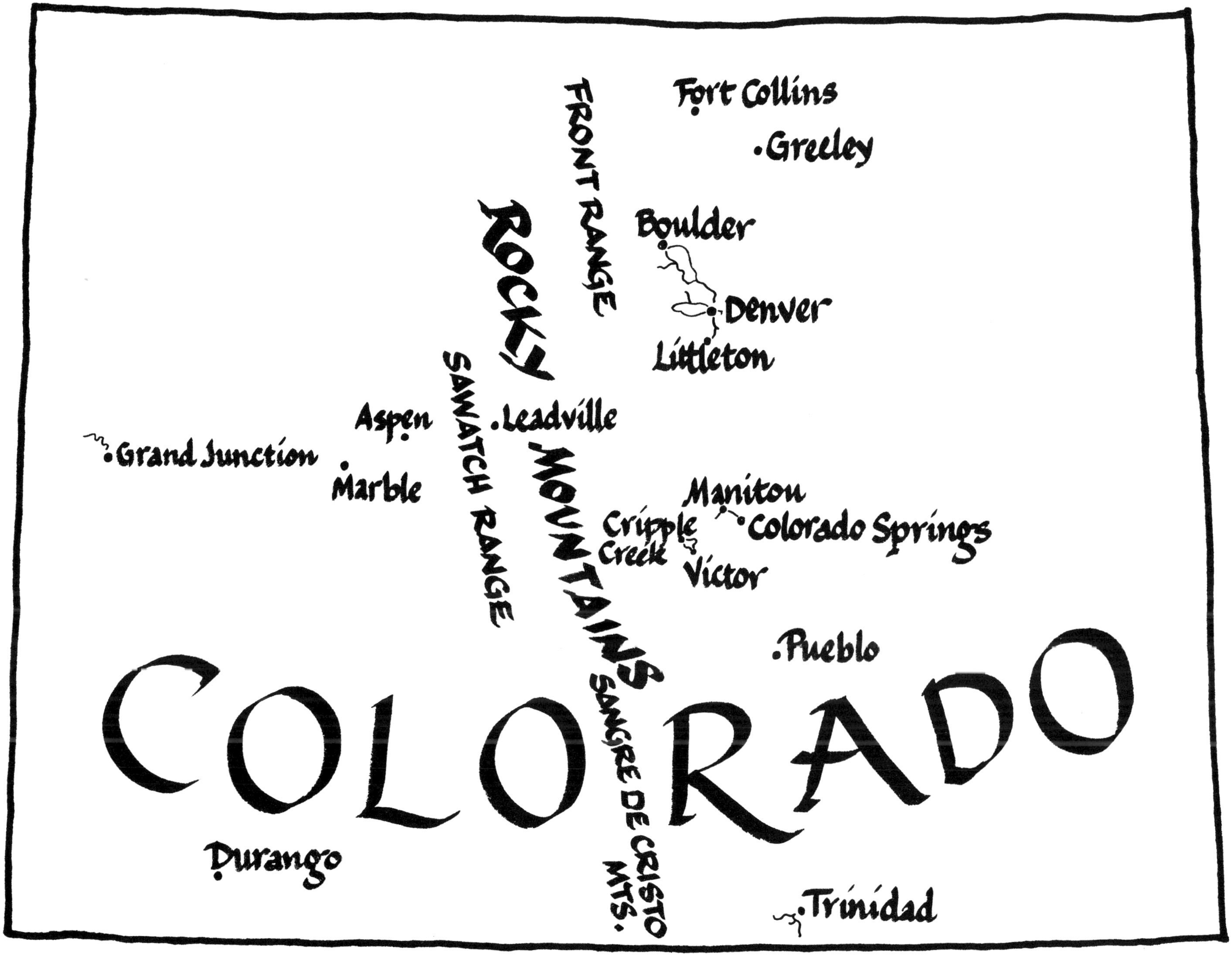

Fort Collins
Greeley
FRONT RANGE
Boulder
ROCKY
Denver
Littleton
SAWATCH RANGE
Aspen
Leadville
Grand Junction
Marble
MOUNTAINS
Manitou
Cripple Creek
Colorado Springs
Victor
Pueblo
SANGRE DE CRISTO MTS.

COLORADO

Durango
Trinidad

CENTENNIAL STATE TROLLEYS

INTRODUCTION

Perfected in the late 1880s by a graduate of the United States Naval Academy, Frank Julian Sprague, the electric streetcar became prolific and by the opening of the twentieth century could be found trundling its way down the streets of almost every American community with a population over fifteen thousand. Preceding it came the horsecar, and to a lesser extent—in cities of some size—a brief flurry of cable cars. But once established, the electric streetcar had no equal until its arch rival—the automobile—entered the picture and became available to the general population.

EVERYTHING'S UP TO DATE IN BOULDER CITY

As the nation expanded and communities sprang up (sometimes in the most unusual geographic locations) the test to maintain a community's existence was constant. To survive, many factors were important, but a primary consideration was location along a well-traveled route. From the beginning of a community's founding, various types of transport played an important role in its economy.

In what appears to be a staged scene, Denver Tramway car 50's motorman glances toward the camera while other company personnel look on. The announcement on the dash indicates that the photo might well have been taken in 1917, shortly after this 1902 product of the Woeber Carriage Company was converted to the Pay-As-You-Enter fare collection system.

Denver Tramway was considered as a progressive company by the industry, and this is reflected in its logo. *(both, Museum collection)*

As towns grew, a place was no place until it could boast of having amenities similar to those of its bigger brothers. And local public transportation was one of the most sought after features, in town after town, all across the country. It was felt by the movers and shakers that their town was not on the map until it had a horsecar line or two. By the middle of the 1800s, or shortly thereafter, as one exited a train station, pride of place was a set of tracks in the center of the street with a bob-tail horsecar (so named because of its entrance at the "tail-end" of the car) waiting to take the prospective passenger uptown to one of the posh hostelries. If you were a local resident, and were not one of the "upper-crust" who could afford a horse and carriage, horsecar lines permitted one the freedom to travel about town or choose a neighborhood befitting your station in life. And to be sure, it beat walking!

Unfortunately, the system was far from perfect. Even a small company with just a few cars required a large number of horses or mules to keep it going. And that particular type of motive power required a lot of oats, created a great deal of obnoxious and odoriferous byproduct along the route, quickly wore out and could easily get sick and die.

GREELEY, COLORADO, TUESDAY EVENING, NOVEMBER 16, 1909

When the Street Cars Come to Greeley

In the name of the business men W. C. Wilson agreed with suggestions already made for the organization of a charitable body and as a merchant saw the great benefit it would be from the standpoint of placing charity where it belongs.

Senator James W. McCreery then arose and at his suggestion the committee looking toward permanency in organization was named.

Support Is Pledged to Fortnightly Club

CATHOLIC FAIR PROSPECTS BRIGHT

MUSIC BENEFIT WILL BE FOR LIBRARY

Frequently the media—upon the introduction of something new to the public—portrays it as a traumatic experience. Five months prior to commencement of electric streetcar operation by the Greeley & Denver Rail Road Company, the *Greeley Tribune's* cartoon characterized its arrival as cause for chaotic confusion on the streets of the town. *(Museum collection)*

DOG PERMIT
..Charge 25 Cents..
OWNER'S RECEIPT
Conductor
05500

1 2 3 4 5 6 7 8 9 10 11 12
05500
TWENTY-FIVE CENTS
DOG PERMIT
Entitling holder to transportation for one Dog on line indicated at extreme right, if presented on date punched.
Wm Lathrop

1 2 3 4 5 6 7 8 9 10 11
12 13 14 15 16 17 18 19 20 21 22
23 24 25 26 27 28 29 30 31

From To
Man
Tej.
Wah.
Sp.
Ins.
N. H.
Cem.
Gf.
Ros.

Progress was steadily on the march and for a time after 1873 the invention of the cable car provided a temporary answer to better serving the public. But, because of its enormous expense, a cable car system was only prudent in those communities where private capital was available in sufficient amounts to pay for its installation. Cable cars were an improvement, because they were not subject to outbreaks of epizootic epidemics, were faster and could pull trailers to accommodate additional riders. But they were not the final answer.

CLANG, CLANG, CLANG GOES THE TROLLEY

Other inventors had tried, but it was not until 1888—in Richmond, Virginia, where Sprague built his first system—that the electric streetcar became dependable and available to the industry. In common with today's Fords and Hondas, skateboards and personal computers, the major reason for the existence of city transport was its ability to make money for its investors. Since no other form of transportation had come on the scene to take its place, the streetcar retained a monopoly in the marketplace. And from the time of its invention until economics changed, the electric streetcar played an important role in everyday life. At its peak, it was

(top) Colorado Springs & Interurban Railway Company's full fare token enlarged to twice its original size. *(Syd Joseph collection)*

(center) Established in 1905 and served by the Broadmoor line of the Colorado Springs & Interurban Railway Company, Little Coney Island and The Zoo was the Springs equivalent to Elitch's Gardens in Denver. The ticket provided the bearer with entrance to the park and transportation on the car line.

(bottom) With proper payment, man's best friend could ride on the streetcars in the Springs, as confirmed by the existence of this ticket. *(both, Museum collection)*

not only used to go back and forth to work but also took the family downtown shopping, to a show at a movie palace, to school, on a picnic or to a relative's final resting place. Everyone used it. "It's the most democratic of vehicles," said William Jennings Bryan when discussing the attributes of the electric streetcar.

To be sure, not all systems that were built were destined to be a success. And a good case could be made that some should not have been built at all. But the American way and its attendant quest for success would prove a strong driving force during the heyday of the streetcar.

FROM A TO V

Colorado's recorded early history is filled with tales of colorful characters who played important roles in the development of the state. Attracted by the chance to gain quick fame and fortune from mining the riches that lay beneath the soil, the first great wave of settlers did not prove to be all that permanent. More bust than boom was to be the fortune of many who came with little else than a pick and shovel in their trunk of belongings. Of those that survived the harshness of reality, many moved on to hoped-for greener pastures.

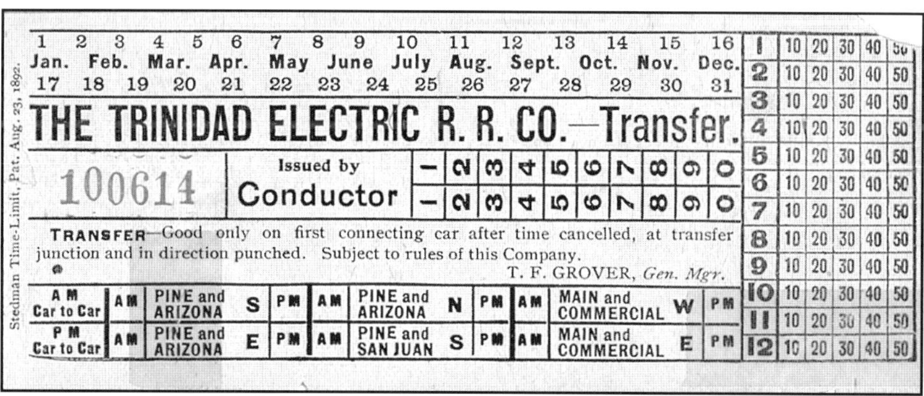

(top) A Sunday ticket from the Denver & Interurban.

(center) A five-cent commutation ticket from the Cripple Creek District interurban.

(bottom) Although patented in 1892 by the Stedmen Company, this style transfer was not used in Trinidad until 1904 when electric streetcar service began. *(all, Museum collection)*

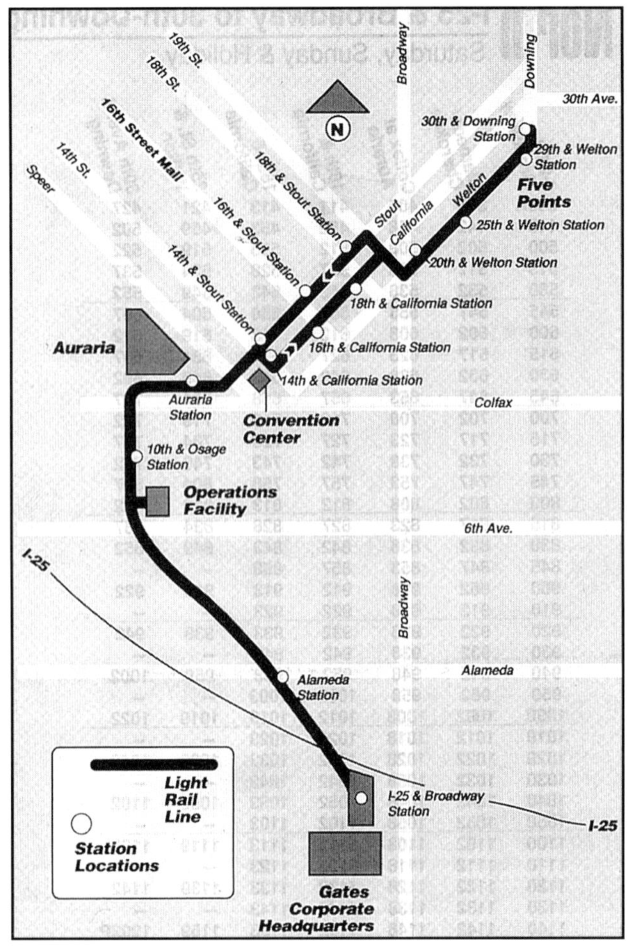

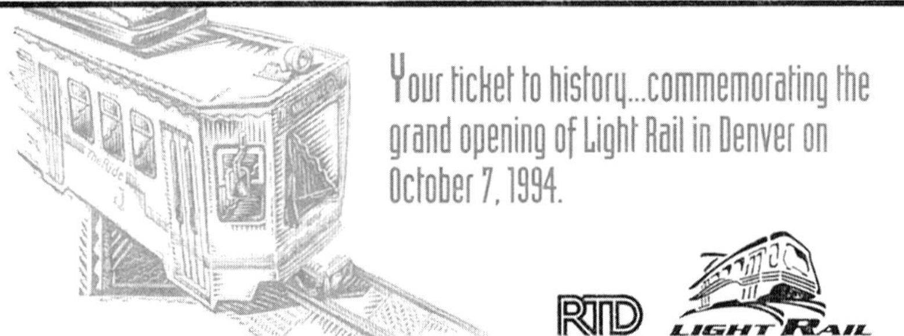

Those who remained, and some did in fact attain those sought-after riches, were sufficient in number to establish settlements that time proved to be permanent. And the towns later became home to those who arrived, in increasing numbers, with the railroad's advancing ribbons of steel.

By 1870, folks in front range towns were of a mind to "keep up with the Joneses," and just before the centennial of the Union some began dabbling in the promotion of local transportation. Denver became the first to establish horsecar service in 1871, with other communities along the front range and throughout the state climbing on board in quick succession. Surprisingly, the mountain communities of Aspen and Leadville saw horsecar service for brief periods. When the electric streetcar was perfected Denver again took the lead in the state followed by Boulder, Colorado Springs, Grand Junction, Greeley, Pueblo, Trinidad, Cripple Creek and Victor. This then, in words and pictures, is the story of the life and times of the streetcar in the Centennial State.

(map) Electric rail service returned to the Centennial State's capital city on October 7, 1994, with the inauguration of the Regional Transportation District's 5.3-mile light rail transit (LRT) line. Eleven Siemens-Duewag type SD-100 articulated light rail vehicles (LRV) are used in daily service from the Five Points area to Broadway and I-25.

(ticket) The proof-of-payment fare system (valid transfer, ticket or pass) is in force when traveling on Denver's LRT line. The reverse side of early single-fare tickets sported wording in reference to commencement of the first of three days of free rides before revenue service began. *(both, author's collection)*

ASPEN

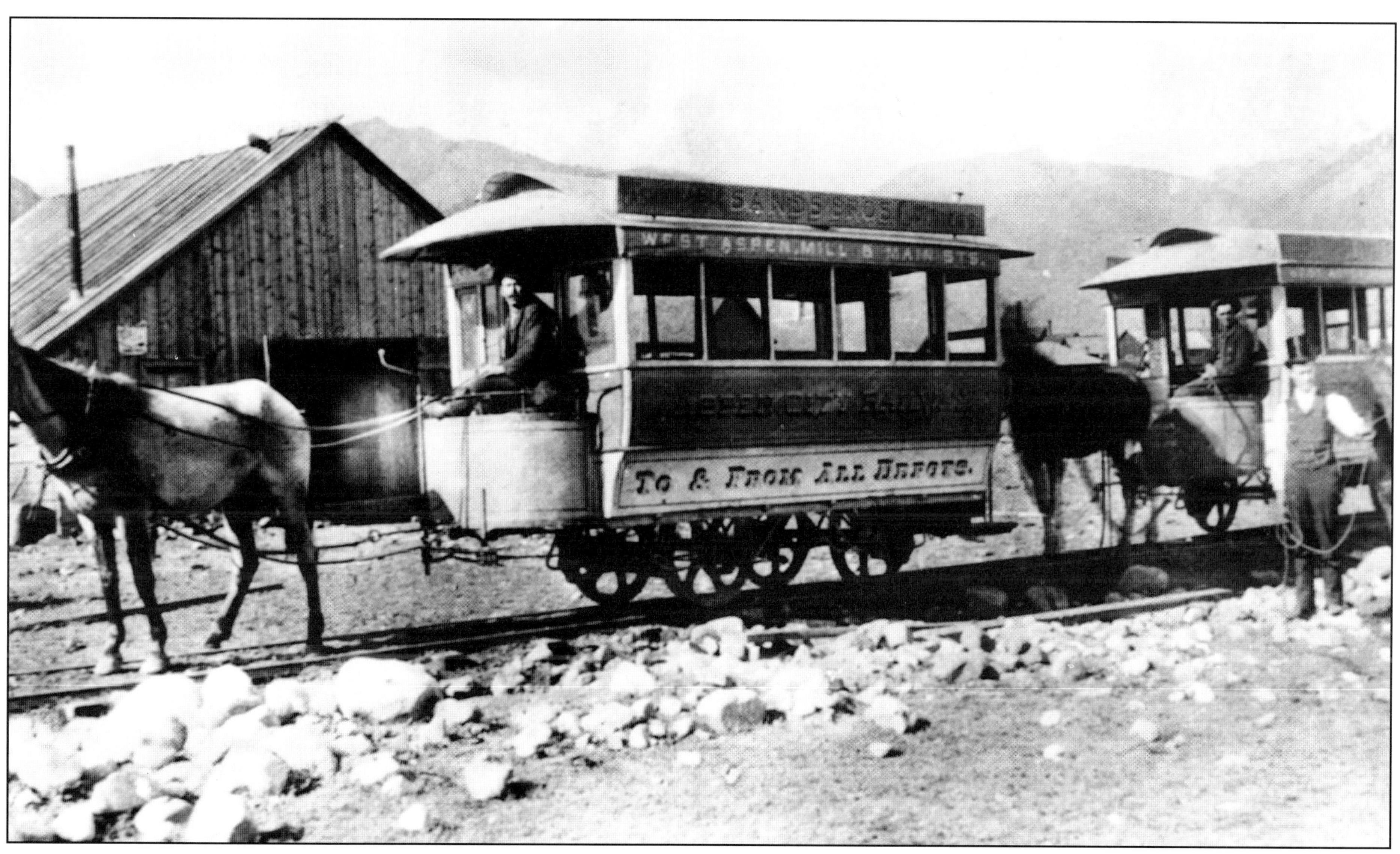

ASPEN

The town of Aspen was founded by those who arrived too late to stake claims in the silver camp of Leadville. Prospecting began in the area in 1878, but it was not until the arrival of the Denver & Rio Grande Railroad in 1887 that things began to boom. During the years 1887 to 1893 the town's population grew from six to twelve thousand people, some being of a pretty rowdy nature, while rich silver ore came down from Aspen and Smuggler mountains. The influx of people caused expansion beyond the city limits, which created a need for some form of transportation.

In September 1889, the city council granted a charter to the Aspen City Railway to build a municipal streetcar line. Although electric streetcars had by this time been perfected and were already operating in Denver, there was no mention of building such a system in Aspen.

The first horsecar arrived in early December 1889, and three weeks later a second car arrived and service began. The completed system eventually totaled somewhat over two miles, stretching from the fairgrounds, through neighborhoods and downtown, to the railroad stations. Charles Hallam advertised his new subdivision with the slogan "Regular Street Car Service Guaranteed." It was not uncommon for a burgeoning community to point with pride to the fact that it had public transport. Aspen was no different.

In 1890 production in the local silver mines was going full-tilt and, with the discovery of some especially rich veins in the Mollie Gibson mine, Aspen finally overtook Leadville as the chief silver producer in Colorado. That would prove short-lived.

(previous page) Here is one of the few known photos showing the two horsecars of the Aspen City Railway. The fare on the short-lived system was five cents to travel anywhere on the line. *(Museum collection)*

In July 1891 the U.S. Congress enacted the Sherman Silver Purchase Act, which required the Treasury Department to buy specific amounts of silver each month at market prices. But because supplies were continually increasing, the market price began to drop. When Great Britain announced that India would no longer mint silver rupees, prices for the ore took a steep dive. By July 1893, along with the announcement that President Cleveland would call for the repeal of the Sherman Act, almost every silver mine in Colorado had closed. Aspen was hard hit, and by the end of the summer the industry work force dropped from 2,250 to 150 miners. Outsiders sent money to establish a relief fund to help the residents. No records have been found regarding the abandonment of the horsecar system, but it is safe to say that it succumbed during this period. It would be a number of years before Aspen would discover a new source of revenue—snow.

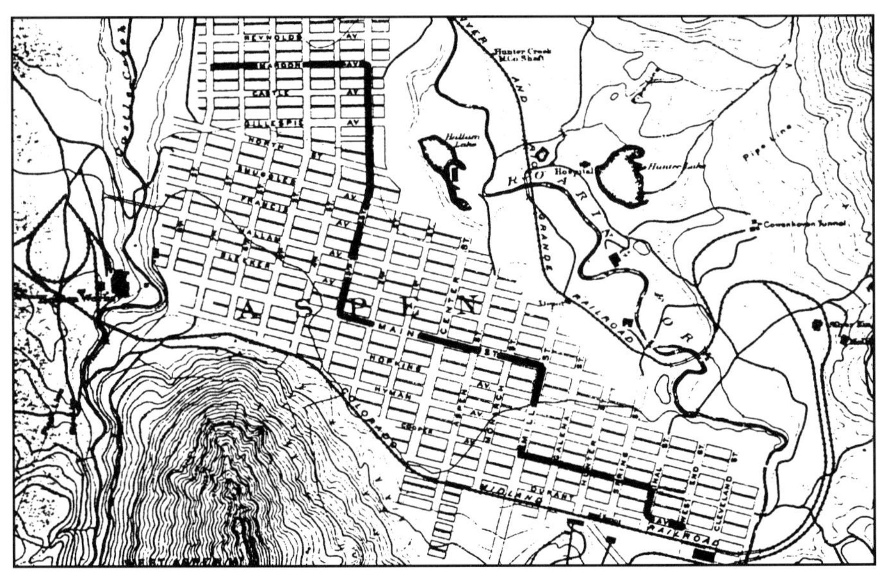

BOULDER

BOULDER

Boulder's formative years were difficult indeed. The first year's crops were eaten by grasshoppers. Unlike many early settlements stores were not established, goods being sold from wagons that passed through the area. Property was sold at exorbitant prices because of gold camps located to the west. Although the first settlers arrived in the vicinity as early as 1858, it was not until the arrival of the railroad in 1873 and establishment of the University of Colorado in 1874-75 that the town began to take on a permanent nature.

In 1872 an unsuccessful attempt was made to start a local street railway, but it was not until 1891 that definite steps were taken. On July 9, 1891, articles of incorporation were filed by the Boulder Railway and Improvement Company, with surprisingly comprehensive objectives, to say the least. It was to buy, sell, exchange, improve and lease real and personal property, erect buildings of all kinds, carry on pleasure resorts, operate clay beds, build and operate all kinds of roads, canals, ditches, reservoirs, water pipes, conduits, telegraph and telephone lines, borrow and lend money, ad infinitum.

Grading began on Pearl Street at Fifth on July 18th and, although the contractor left Boulder on August 3rd with the funds that were set aside to pay the workers, matters were quickly settled by the manager. The first horsecar arrived on September 13th and operated over the completed portion. Although there were high hopes for success, the company was not well financed, and the next day the little company was reorganized. The line struggled along but to no avail. On February 20, 1892, the equipment was sold by the sheriff, the horsecar became a lunch wagon, and the tracks were torn up.

Six years later, in 1898, a new group of promoters entered the scene, this time to construct an electric streetcar system. Receiving city council approval, construction began in 1899, and on June 23rd the last work on the line was completed. Eleven cars, which came second hand from Denver, made up the roster and the line opened on June 24th at 7 a.m. On the first day 6,000 fares were collected.

With the exception of one early spectacular accident, the system served the community well. In 1914 the property was taken over by Western Light & Power Company (part of Public Service Company of Colorado after 1922) and spent the rest of its life going about the business of providing service between the University, downtown and the northern neighborhoods. The cars made their final runs on June 2, 1931, when the entire system was replaced by buses.

(previous page) Company personnel stand at attention next to a trio of Boulder's early streetcars grouped in front of the carhouse that was located at 12th and Arapahoe (now Broadway). *(Carnegie Branch Library for Local History, Boulder)*

Car 203, purchased second hand from Denver Tramway, is being unloaded from a railroad flatcar at 12th and Water(now Broadway and Canyon). A makeshift unloading ramp of ties and a curved section of rail has been put in place, and the car is being pushed down the incline by the gentleman in the hat and white shirt, while two others are on the front platform. We hope one is cranking the handbrake to prevent the car from running away. A contingent of youngsters is seated on sections of unused rail while other townsfolk are scattered about, all witnessing a piece of history unfold on June 23, 1899. *(Carnegie Branch Library for Local History, Boulder Historical Society collection)*

(above) *(above)* Boulder City was originally named for the numerous large stones in the vicinity, and it seems that this picture was taken to prove the point! A streetcar and its trailer are posed amid the “boulders” near the Chautauqua in 1899. *(Denver Public Library Western History Department)*

(right) Car 202 waits next to Bowen’s Hotel at 13th and Walnut during the period when tracks circled the block bounded by 13th and 14th, Walnut and Water streets. *(Museum collection)*

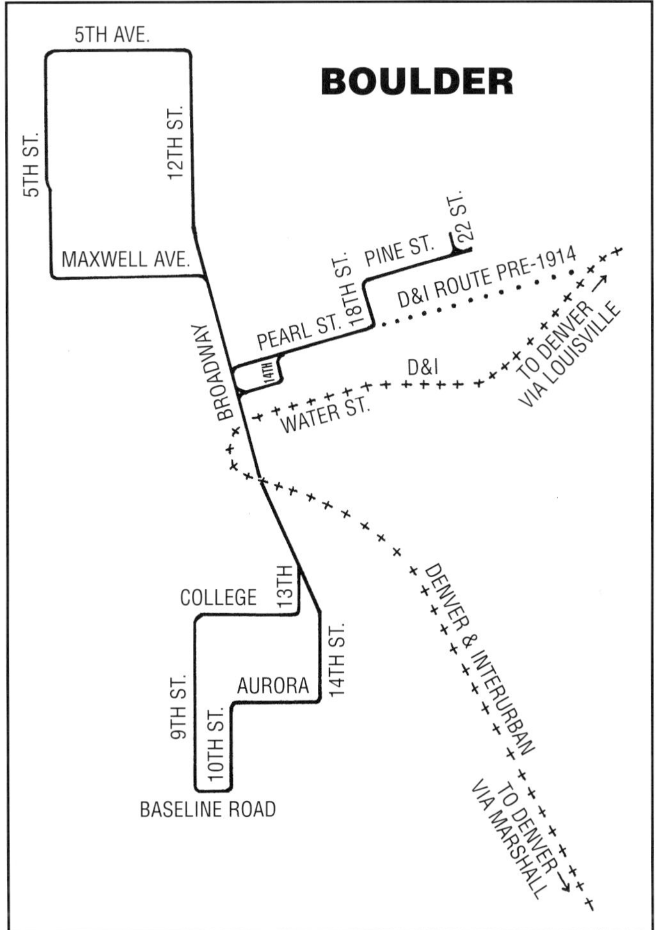

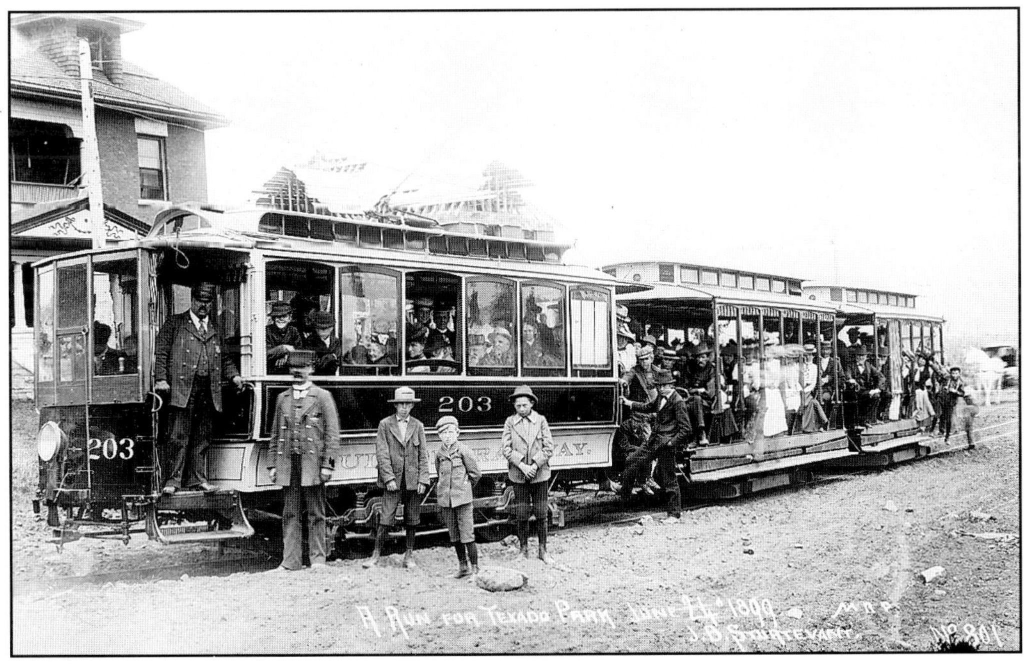

(above left) Three cars are posed at Walnut and 12th with the operators lined up for the photographer. Note that two gauges of track show plainly. The city car lines were built to 42-inch gauge with standard gauge (four-feet, eight-and-a-half inches) provided for the Denver & Interurban. *(E.J. Haley collection)*

(left) Motor 203, two trailers, passengers and interested spectators pose for the camera on the first day of operation, June 24, 1899, on a run to Texado Park. *(J.B. Sturtevant photo, E.J. Haley collection)*

The map shows local Boulder car lines with dash lines representing the final route of the Denver & Interurban.

(left) This photograph almost seems like a still out of a Laurel and Hardy movie. Ollie is saying to Stan, "Here's another nice mess you've gotten me into." Well, it is a fine mess considering that the streetcar went off the end of the track, landed in the mucky gumbo and did what kids of today would call a "wheelie." *(Museum collection)*

(right) This is not the way to take care of a streetcar! The system's most spectacular accident occurred on July 4, 1902, near Mount St. Gertrude's Academy. The car and its trailer were jammed with riders when the brakes failed on the steep hill and both left the rails on the curve at the bottom. Although the streetcar was totally demolished, only one fatality was recorded along with 20 people injured. *(J.B. Sturtevant photo, E.J. Haley collection)*

(left) During most of the era of the electric streetcar in Boulder the trolleys came second hand from Denver and embodied a motley selection. This 300-series car was originally two separate vehicles, spliced together and operated by Denver Tramway before being sold to Boulder. *(Carnegie Branch Library for Local History, Boulder Historical Society)*

(below left) Car 3 is at an unknown location. The roof line is unusual and sometimes referred to as an "umbrella" or "balloon" roof.

(below) A motorman and one of his passengers pose with car 21. The advertisement on the fender dates this photo to circa 1917-18. *(both, Carnegie Branch Library for Local History, Boulder)*

The system in Boulder eventually purchased new equipment. In 1917, cars 1, 2 and 3 arrived from the American Car Company of St. Louis, and No. 4 was delivered in 1922. They were all safety cars but were not recognized as Birneys by the industry. Not until the final car, No. 5, was purchased in 1923 did the system have a true Birney. In this view, Boulder Street Railway's 1 and 2 prepare to pass one another in a photo taken during the last year of operation, 1931. *(E.J. Haley collection)*

COLORADO SPRINGS

COLORADO SPRINGS

There is a street in the "Springs" called Wood Avenue which locals once called "Millionaire Row." It was on this avenue that those who made their fortunes from the Cripple Creek mines built their palatial mansions. That is to say, all except one — Winfield Scott Stratton — who became prominently involved with the local street railway.

The "Springs" (as it is called by residents) had its beginnings through the foresight of General William Jackson Palmer, promoter of the Denver & Rio Grande Railway. He was a man who made and unmade towns by directing where the tracks were laid. The general was taken by the sight of the nearby mountains and foothill canyons, and he directed his company to purchase 10,000 acres of land at the site of what would become Colorado Springs. On July 31, 1871, the first stake was driven at what is now the southeast corner of Pikes Peak and Cascade avenues. Three months later his narrow gauge railroad line reached the town from Denver.

During its first years the town was known as Fountain Colony because of its position on Fountain Creek, but later it was renamed Colorado Springs for the mineral springs at the nearby village of Manitou. Lot deeds contained a clause prohibiting the manufacture or sale of intoxicating liquors on the premises. This restriction lasted until 1933, when prohibition was repealed.

The first building served as Palmer's office, railroad depot and post office. In 1871 the foundations of the Colorado Springs Hotel were begun, and by the end of the year more than 150 structures had been built, many of them portable houses shipped from Chicago. The railroad publicized the region as a "scenic wonderland," and within a short time the Garden of the Gods, Seven Falls, Cheyenne Mountain and the springs at Manitou were almost as well known as Pikes Peak.

In 1882 the Antlers Hotel and a new opera house opened, and in 1885 the Colorado Midland Railway began its push westward from the city. In 1887 the Colorado Springs & Manitou Street Railway was organized and opened a horsecar line on Tejon Street from downtown north to Cache la Poudre Street. The following year work began on a line west to Colorado City. It ran northwest on Colorado Avenue as far as 28th Street and opened on May 15, 1889. Also in 1889 the city was chosen as the western terminus of the Chicago, Rock Island & Pacific Railway. By September 1889, the Tejon line was extended north as far as Van Buren Street. The horse railway was purchased in 1890, became the Colorado Springs Rapid Transit Railway Company and was converted to electric operation. This company relaid all of the existing rail and completed an extension from Colorado City to Manitou Springs which opened on October 30, 1890. The next year the cog railway was built to the summit of Pikes Peak.

(previous page) Three Colorado Springs & Interurban Railway Birneys (112, 116 and 109) gather on Pikes Peak Avenue circa 1925. It is unknown as to what the poster "It's Up To YOU!" refers to, but the one advertising the silent movie at the Rialto, *Cobra,* starring screen idol Rudolph Valentino, helps date this picture. *(Museum collection)*

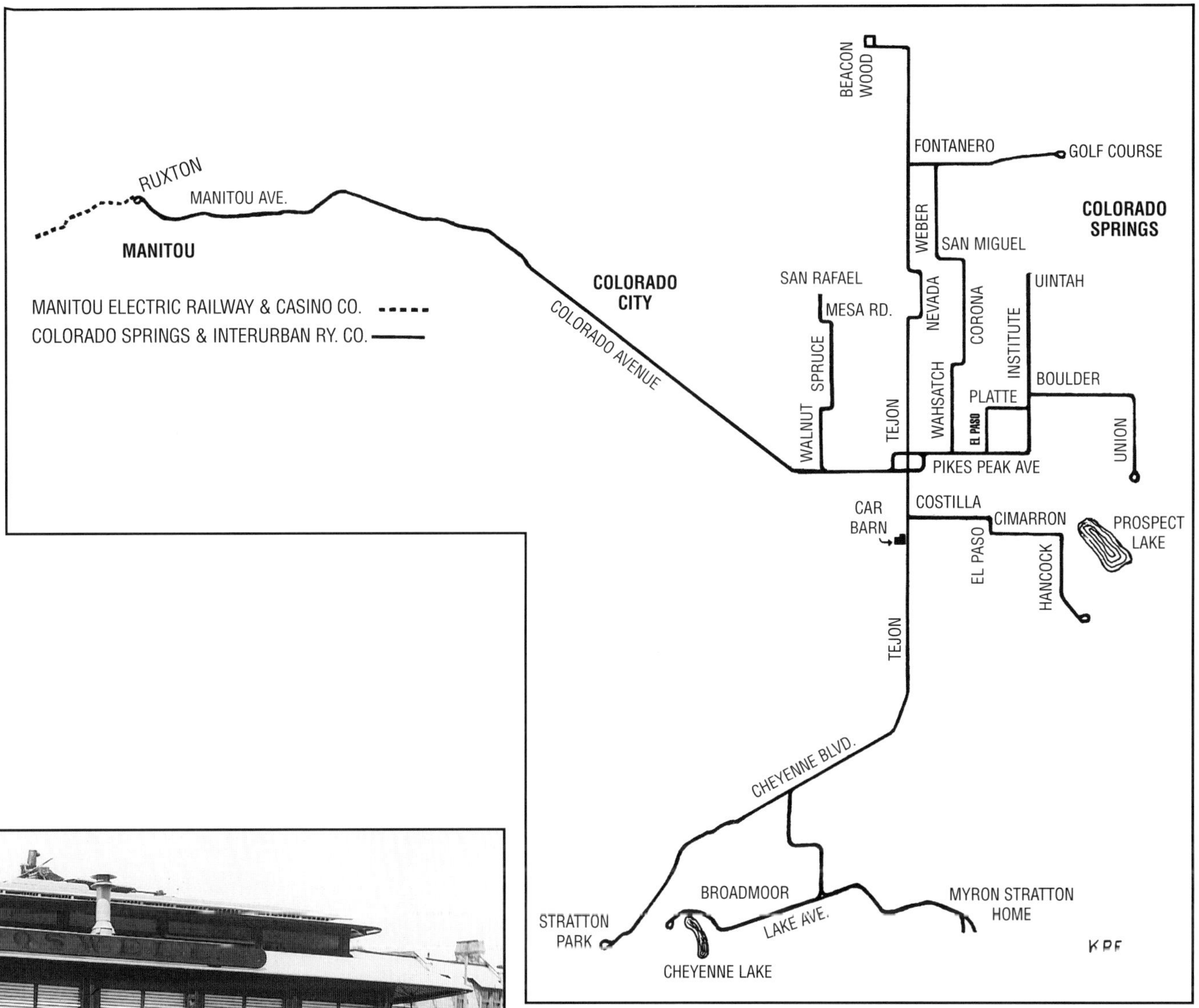

Built by the Pullman Company, car 16 epitomized the craftsmanship of the 1890s. The interior had patterned plush seats, a stove to keep passengers comfy, slatted blinds and highly polished varnished wood. *(both, E.J. Haley collection)*

A trolley car and trailer 12 travel up the avenue toward the original Antlers Hotel about 1896. *(Standley photo, E.J. Haley collection)*

PIKES PEAK AVENUE

A 50-series car, built by Laclede in 1901, moves toward the "new" Antlers Hotel. The original had burned on October 1, 1898. *(George L. Beam photo, E.J. Haley collection)*

THE CARPENTER'S TROLLEY

Enter one of the world's richest miners, Winfield Scott Stratton. By 1889, Colorado Springs society began to take note of just how much a flamboyant philanthropist this ex-carpenter was. He was not at all like General Palmer who, it was said, created the community for love of a woman and to express his acute sense of order and dignity. He was not like the obstreperous James John Hagerman, who built the Colorado Midland to upstage his enemies, nor was he like the notorious Count James Pourtales who catered to snob appeal. Stratton gave of his vast wealth freely, to employees, the Salvation Army and families in need of a home. He even provided bicycles to be distributed among the laundresses of the community.

His glance fell upon the current operation of the transit system in the Springs, and he decided that he could do better. In 1901 he purchased the system and incorporated the Colorado Springs & Interurban Railway. He then proceeded to rebuild, add new lines and purchase new equipment.

Car 76, a 14-bench open model built by Brill in 1901, passes through the sylvan setting of Stratton Park in 1905. Winfield Stratton purchased the 20-acre site for $40,000, pledged $5,000 a year for maintenance, $4,000 for Colorado Midland Band concerts every summer Sunday and $4,000 a year for dance music. The park opened on June 6, 1901. *(Colorado Historical Society)*

When completed, the new system totaled some 41 miles: out Wahsatch and Institute streets, east to Prospect Lake, to the race track at Roswell and to the Loop at Manitou Springs, where it connected with the cars of the Manitou Electric Railway & Casino Company. Stratton purchased 20 acres of Dixon's ranch, located at the wooded junction of North and South Cheyenne Creeks, and created Stratton Park on the new second car line to Broadmoor along Cheyenne Creek. The grounds were landscaped, ponds were created, a band shell was built and picnic and playground areas were added. The new streetcars, painted in a resplendent olive green, became the pride of the city.

Ultimately, Stratton spent two million dollars rehabilitating and extending the system and lived long enough to see it become a success. By the summer of 1902 capacity and service had improved to such an extent that, for the first time since 1894, the company was earning a profit.

Known for his large consumption of alcohol, he died from complications due to cirrhosis of the liver and diabetes on September 14, 1902. At 2 P.M. on the day of his funeral, every streetcar in operation came to a standstill for five minutes in honor of its benefactor.

Because of a vast amount of litigation, Stratton's last dream did not become a reality until ten years after his death. His will directed his estate to be used for the construction and maintenance of a home for dependent children and elderly poor. It was to be named in honor of his father, Myron Stratton, with income from his various holdings paying for the home's operating expenses.

Operation of the streetcar system was turned over to the trustees of his estate, who in turn continued to expand and improve the company. A new extension was opened from a junction with the Wahsatch line, and additional cars were constructed in the company shops. In 1917-1918 new trackage was put into service to the Myron Stratton Home from a connection with the Broadmoor line at Seventh and Lake.

(above right) Car 65 (built in the company shops in 1906-07) heads north on Tejon Street at Pikes Peak Avenue. The intersection was known as The Busy Corner. The Exchange National Bank, at the time the tallest building in the Springs, appears on the left and the First National Bank is on the right. *(Tutt Library)*

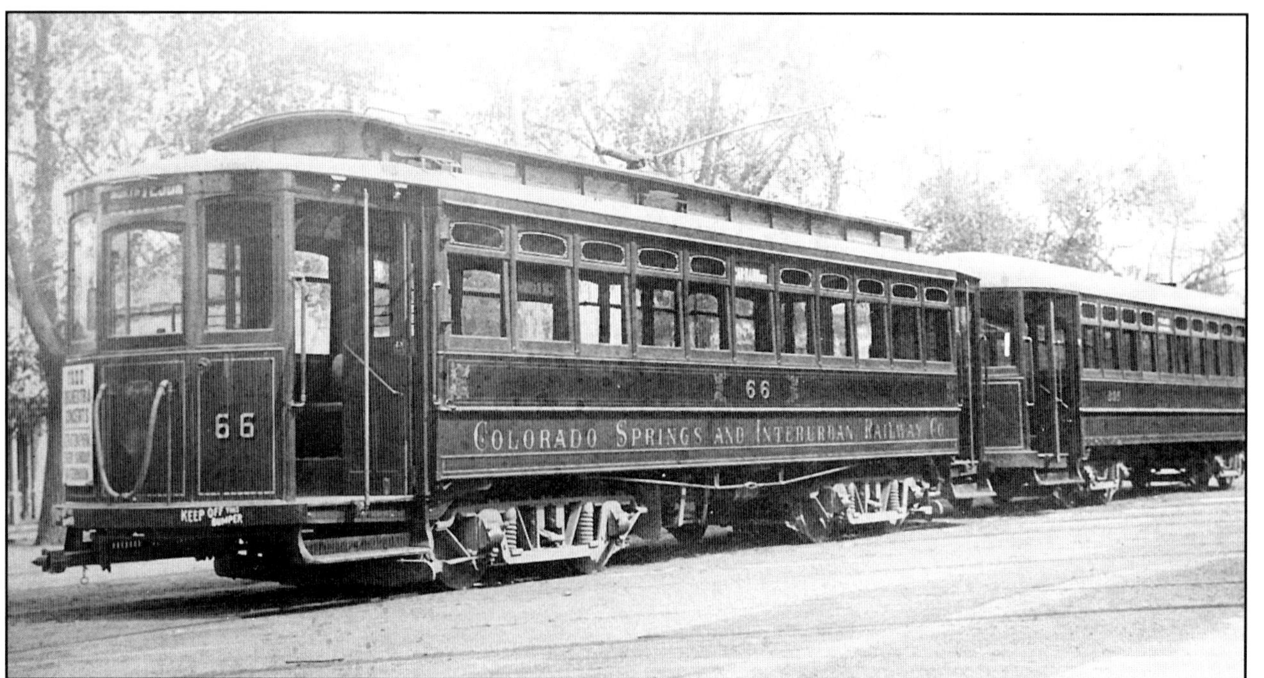

(right) Streetcar 66 and trailer 265 pose for the camera at the Tejon St. barn. Both cars were built by the company. *(both E.J. Haley collection)*

(right) One could think that a Hollywood production crew had a hand in hanging the icicles from car 62. Winters along the Front Range are usually mild affairs, compared to what other parts of the country receive, but every now and then an upslope wind can cause a large deposit of snow, as shown in this post-1921 scene on Pikes Peak Avenue at Tejon. *(Museum collection)*

(below) Car 60 has arrived in Manitou Springs, circa 1909. The conical roofed buildings in the foreground house the Cheyenne and Navajo springs, the ornate building at left is for Soda Spring and the large structure behind the trees is the Cliff House. *(L.C.McClure photo, E.J. Haley collection)*

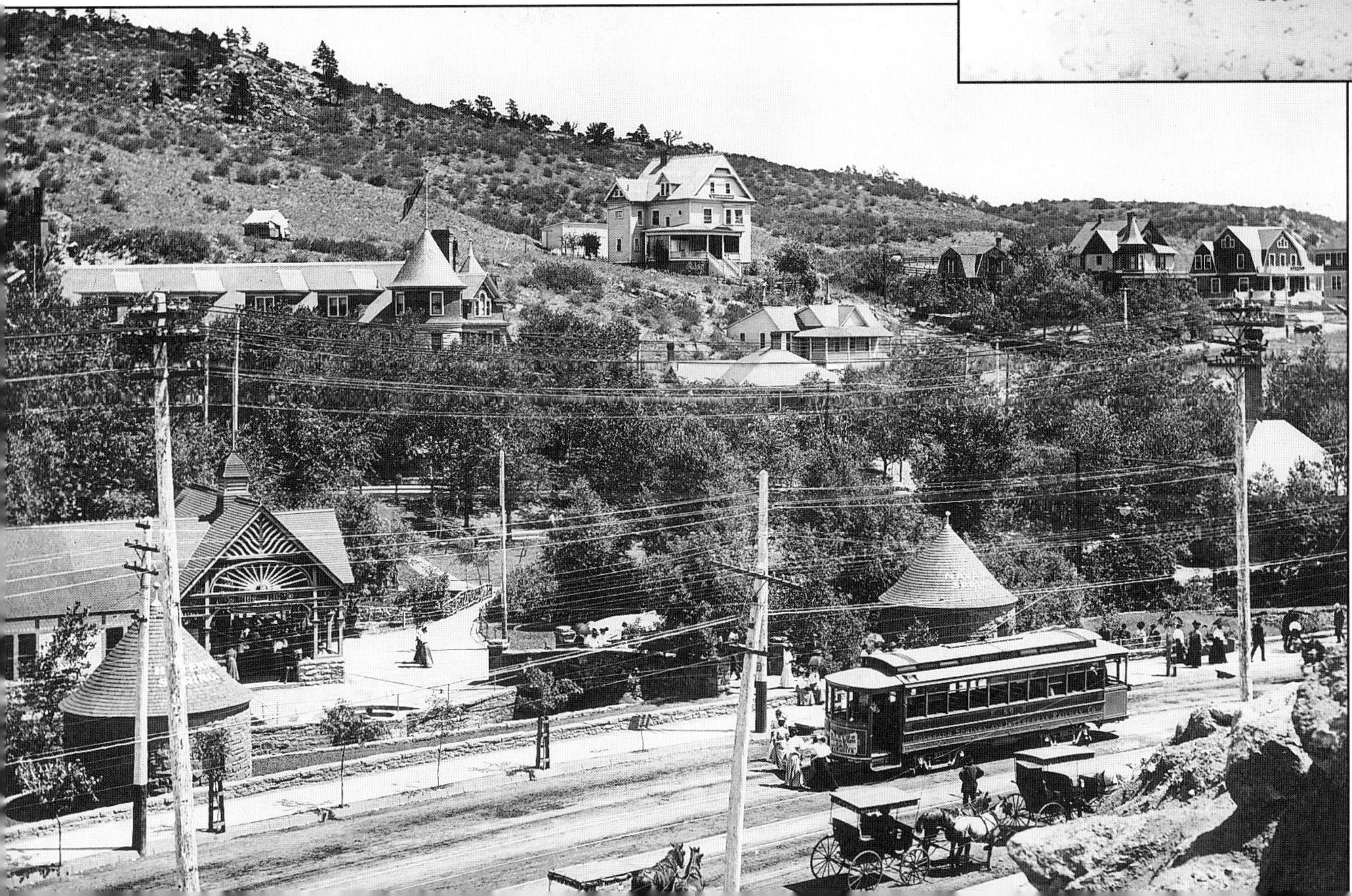

Birney 102 is eastbound on Pikes Peak Avenue circa 1925, with an ad for the movie *The Crowded Hour*, which was showing at the Rialto Theater. The second Antlers Hotel, which stood from 1901 to 1964, is at the foot of the avenue with Pikes Peak looming in the background. *(Standley photo, E.J. Haley collection)*

This children's fare token from the Colorado Springs & Interurban Railway is illustrated at double its actual size. *(Syd Joseph collection)*

(left) A Birney Safety Car proceeds north on Tejon at Kiowa during the last years of operation. *(Standley photo, E.J. Haley collection)*

(below) Car 62 became a roadside diner, the Red Onion, in Green Mountain Falls after the abandonment of the system. *(E.J. Haley collection)*

THE END OF THE LINE

Although the system was maintained in excellent condition, the inroads of automobile use would affect ridership as it did in communities across the country. Little by little, lines with light ridership were abandoned. New and more efficient single-truck streetcars were purchased but to no avail. On April 30, 1932, Stratton's splendid contribution to the street railway industry and his community was replaced by the rubber tired buses of the Colorado Springs Bus Company.

Thirty-five Birney Safety Cars were purchased by the system. Car 108 was from a group of 11 that was built by the American Car Company of St. Louis in 1918. The other 24 came from Cincinnati Car Company in 1919, and these were sold to the Pueblo system in 1935. This scene was at the loop near the Union Printers Home and Hospital in the Nob Hill district, circa 1920. *(Museum collection)*

CRIPPLE CREEK DISTRICT

CRIPPLE CREEK DISTRICT

The state's last great mining boom began in the early 1890s in the Cripple Creek District west of Colorado Springs. By 1900 more than 55,000 people lived in the district. Cripple Creek, with a population of 25,000, was the fourth largest community in the state, followed by Victor with over 18,000 residents. The area between the two towns became dotted with mining camps and small communities, and the need for dependable and frequent transportation became a necessity as the boom set in.

Originally incorporated as the Cripple Creek District Railway, to supplement suburban service provided by the steam railroads of the area, the electric line eventually operated two distinct divisions. The 9.9-mile "high line," opened in 1898, ran from Cripple Creek up a 7.5 percent grade through Poverty Gulch, reaching an altitude of 10,487 feet at Midway. It then passed the Portland Mine and came down Battle Mountain into Victor. The fare was five cents.

In 1899 the system was purchased by the Colorado Springs & Cripple Creek District Railway. This standard gauge steam railroad completed a second electric route, the 5.6-mile "low line," from Cripple Creek to Victor via Elkton in 1901. In the following year, both ends of the high line were rerouted, thereby lengthening it to 12 miles. In 1905, all railroads in the area were united under common management, known as the Allied Lines, which also operated the interurban.

The two routes were heavily used by miners, commuters and shoppers, as well as by tourists who appreciated the exceptional scenery traversed. Half-hourly service was provided on the low line with a ten cent fare, while hourly service was maintained on the high line at a 20 cent fare. "Circle Tour" tickets sold for 25 cents. The line's seven interurban cars and three trailers were all built by Barney & Smith of Dayton, Ohio.

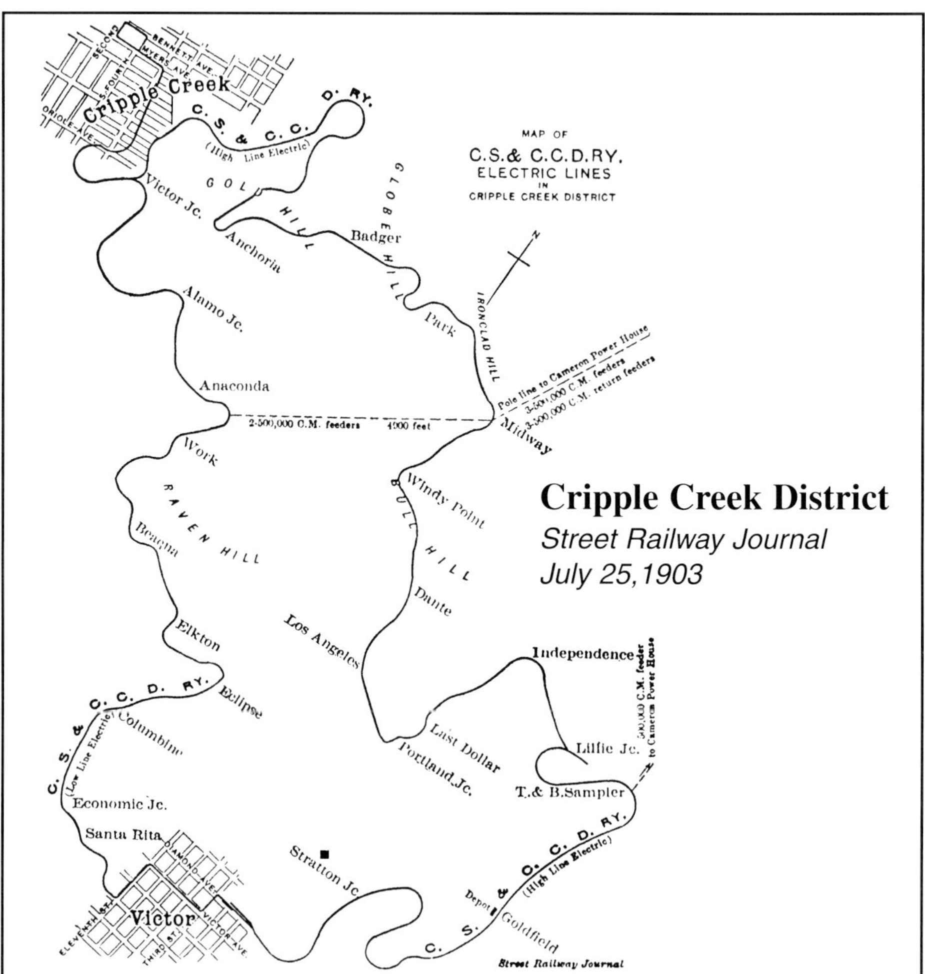

During World War I, mining was cut back, the population declined and service over the high line was reduced to once every two hours and to hourly on the low line. On November 21, 1919, fire destroyed the carbarn and six of the seven motor cars, bringing an abrupt halt to all service. The remaining interurban car was dismantled the next year.

(previous page) On its way to Cripple Creek, car M-105 makes a photo stop just west of Alamo Junction on the low line. *(A.J. Harlan photo, E.J. Haley collection)*

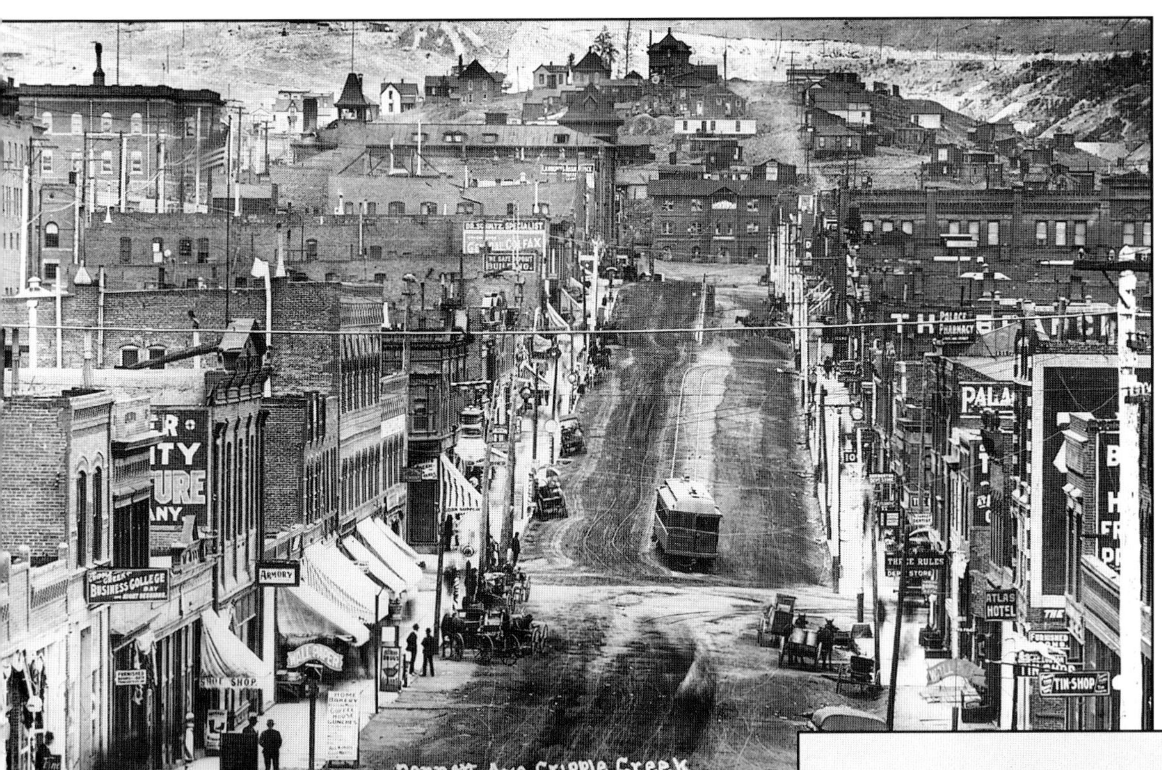

CRIPPLE CREEK
Car M-201 rounds the corner off Bennett Avenue onto Second Street as it departs for Victor via the high line about 1908. In the center distance, at the end of Bennett Avenue, stands the three-story Midland Terminal station, which is now a museum. *(E.J. Haley collection)*

VICTOR
At a crest on Victor Avenue at Fifth Street, an interurban waits for its scheduled departure to Cripple Creek via the low line. *(Huff photograph of Victor Avenue, Mazzulla collection, Amon Carter Museum, Fort Worth, Texas)*

Kids flock to the crossing at Midway to watch the *Evelyn* pass by. The unusual half enclosed, half open platform was unique to the interurbans built for the line. *(E.J. Haley collection)*

Interurban M-106 is on Victor Avenue at Fourth Street in Victor, waiting to depart on the low line for Cripple Creek. *(Don Robertson collection)*

The first four cars built for the line were named instead of numbered. The *Emily* grinds up the 7.5 percent grade in Poverty Gulch, just east of Cripple Creek, on the original high line. This part of the line was abandoned in 1902 and rerouted. The Gold King Mine sits high on the slope of Tenderfoot Hill just above the large pine tree. *(Yelton photo, E.J. Haley collection)*

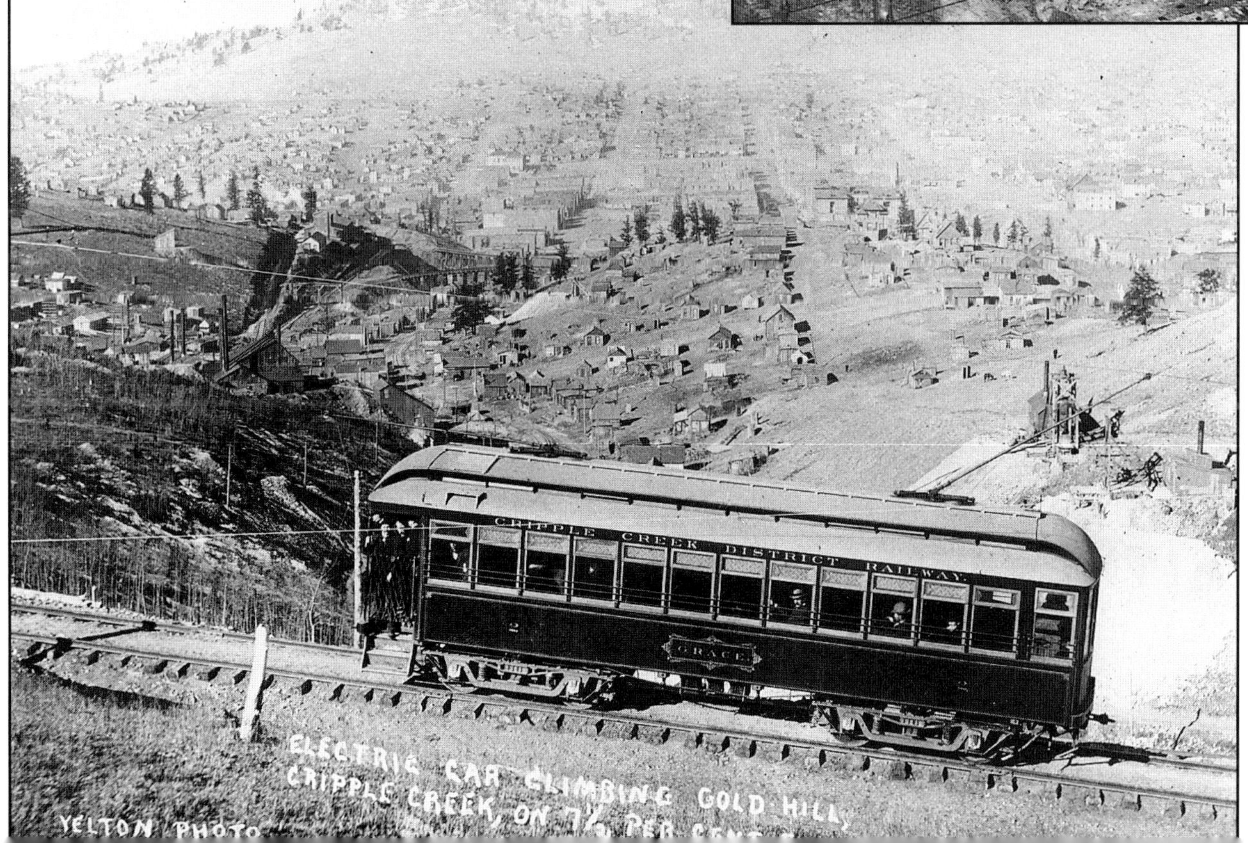

Grace poses on the 7.5 percent grade on the west slope of Gold Hill, high above Cripple Creek. In 1902 the line was rerouted over a less steep alignment. *(Yelton photo, E.J. Haley collection)*

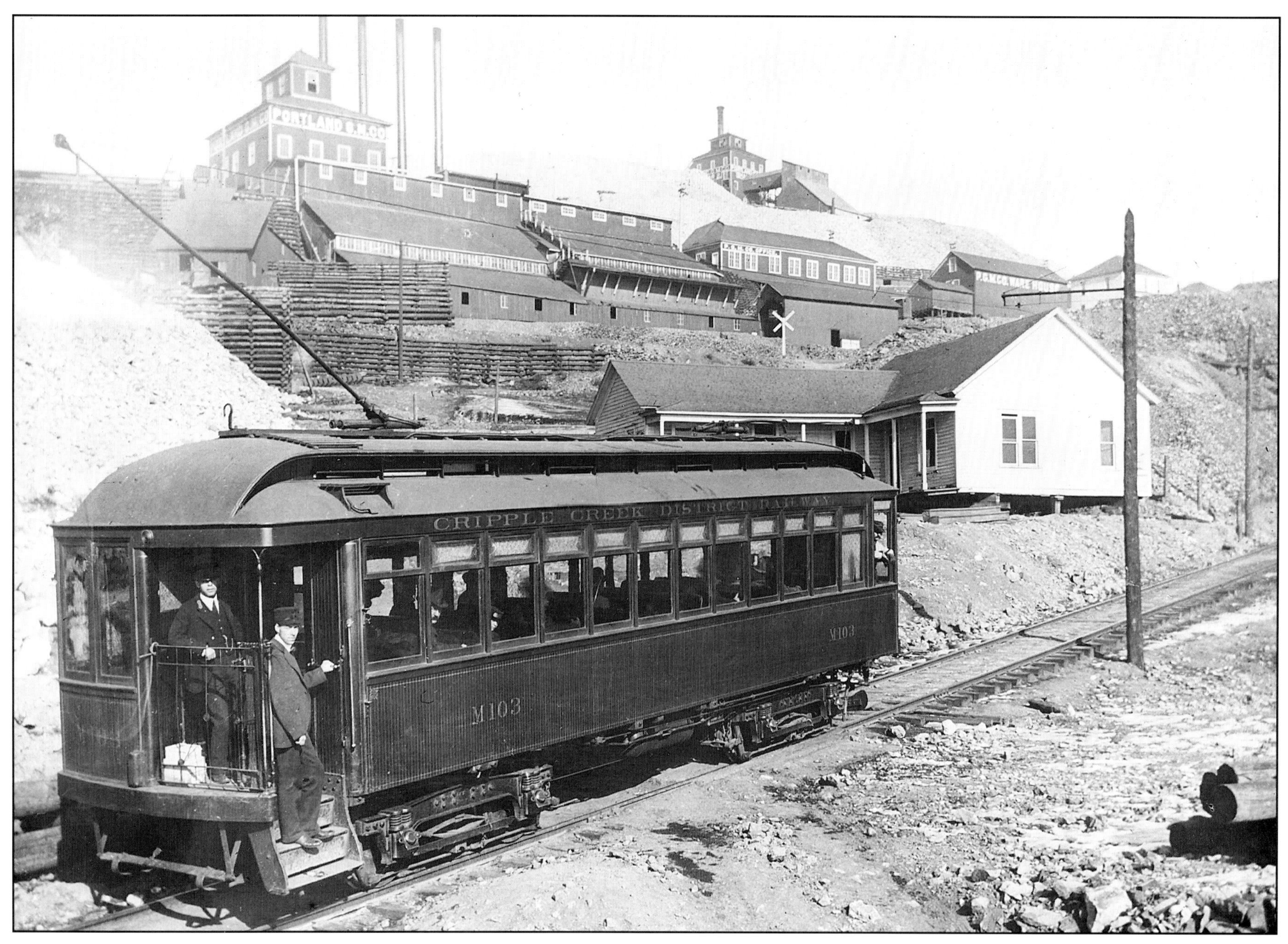

Interurban M-103 ascends the seven percent grade out of Victor, near Portland Junction, as it heads toward Cripple Creek via Midway. Midway, at 10,487 feet, was the highest elevation ever reached by an interurban line in the United States. Portland Mine Nos. 1 and 2 are high on Battle Mountain in the background. An easier but longer grade replaced this section of the line in 1902. *(A.J. Harlan photo, E.J. Haley collection)*

DENVER

HENRY GEORGE
Coca-Cola
Carter Bros
301 HARDWARE 303
Carter Bros
HARDWARE
HOTEL KITCHEN OUTFITS WROUGHT
1262. 16TH. DENVER ~
PHOTO. BY McCLURE.

DENVER

GROWING UP

Dirt streets, hitching posts, bars and bordellos, nickelodeons, the clip-clop of horses' hooves and rattle of wagons and carriages, shouts of whoa and gitty-up. These were the sights and sounds of a young community on the move.

It would not be long before the demand for some sort of public transportation came into being as the town spread out. Horsecars came in 1871, cable cars in 1888, and one year later electric streetcars were introduced on South Broadway.

Paved streets and traffic signs, restaurants and movie palaces, record players and trolley gongs. All the commotion—the result of city life spreading out into the streetcar suburbs.

ONE OF THE BEST

The Denver Tramway Company led the way as it constructed over 260 miles of city trackage and an additional 40 miles of interurban lines to front range communities. In its day, the Tramway was one of the best in the country, with the distinction of having the fastest system-wide schedules of any urban operation. The use of trailer cars increased capacity during rush hours, and the establishment of the "Central Loop" brought most of the 31 car lines into the heart of the business district. With the exception of the very early streetcars and a few interurbans, all cars were home-built by either the Woeber Carriage Company or by the Tramway in its own shops.

Not until 1928 was the bus considered as an adjunct or replacement for the streetcar. Up until 1940 it replaced only a few cross-town and light feeder carlines or was introduced into newer areas.

ROAD KILL

An improved and expanded public road system that fostered the increased use of the private automobile along with changing economics, brought the private transit company to its knees. Financially unable to purchase new streetcars the Tramway opted to replace the entire system with buses. Dash signs began appearing with a caricature of a tearful streetcar, and the words "Good-bye Old Friends," as one after another the lines were abandoned. The streetcar faded into the history books as the last runs were made during the summer of 1950.

PICTURES FROM THE PAST

Following are scenes of a Denver that used to be. Brief stories from an earlier time tell about the streetcar that became as integral a part of everyday life as the automobile is today. The streetcars are long gone, as are most of the structures, but the memories linger on.

(previous page) To a person today, this scene of downtown Denver is almost unrecognizable. With few exceptions, all the buildings in this view looking down 16th Street from Court Place are no longer standing. The large expanse of grass and park fronts the Arapahoe County Court House, which was demolished in 1935. *(L.C. McClure photo, Denver Public Library Western History Department)*

Pedestrians cross 17th Street at Larimer as horsecars converge on the scene. Colorado Midland Railroad has offices on the right and Union Depot is in the background. A writer in the 1870s said the following about the horsecar system, "The street railway is a potent factor in the prosperity of the city. It has given value to outside property, and has enabled men of small means to locate themselves in homes of their own on the outskirts of the town. Nor should its moral influence be overlooked. Strangers coming here with very vague impressions of Denver's status as a metropolitan city, are always favorably impressed by the sight of a well-loaded streetcar rattling along past them, and are ready to admit that the Queen City of the Plains has some genuine and undisputed claims to a place among cities of the first class, East or West. Thanks to the enterprise and liberality of the management, the cars are always neat and clean and comfortable, and only the best `motive power' and the most gentlemanly drivers are employed. As a consequence, no complaints are heard from the patrons of the line, and it is a pleasure instead of a discomfort to ride in the cars of the Denver City Railway Company." *(Denver Public Library Western History Department)*

CABLE CAR DAYS

Two competing companies built several miles of cable car lines in the city. While men are working on a sewer project, at 18th and Larimer, a grip car and trailer of the Denver City Cable Railway Company has just passed by.

The elaborate Windsor Hotel, opened on June 23, 1880, dominates the scene. It was built on the site of the residence of J.H. Kehler, pioneer sheriff of Arapahoe County, which was the second brick building in "Denver City." The Windsor had at least 14 different window shapes, each floor a unit with its own type of window detailing. The hotel closed in early 1958 and was torn down in November 1959. A senior citizen highrise presently occupies the site. (Colorado Historical Society)

(above) A cable car and its trailer proceed up 16th Street at Welton, passing the Masonic Building, which was designed by noted early Denver architect Frank E. Edbrooke and dedicated on July 3, 1890. In the early 1980s, it suffered from an arsonist's torch but has been restored. The next structure, the Kittredge Building rising seven stories, is built of granite and lava rock and was completed in 1890. *(William Henry Jackson photo, E.J. Haley collection)*

At left, the Boston Block (somewhat modified but still standing at 17th & Champa) was built of Colorado red sandstone and opened in 1889. The 17th Street cable line was originally built by the Denver City Cable Railway. *(Colorado Historical Society)*

THE CHANGING SCENE

In Jerome Smiley's *History of Denver*, he stated that the People's Bank Building (erected in 1890 and located on the south corner of 16th and Lawrence) replaced a "...motley collection of small frame structures of little historical interest and less value." The massive structure, designed by Frank E. Edbrooke, was built of Colorado red sandstone and dark red pressed brick. The handsome building was demolished on November 15, 1970, and replaced by the new Central Bank Building. The photo also shows a set of Denver City Cable Railway cars on 16th and, just barely visible to the right, a trailer of the Denver Tramway's Lawrence Street electric line. The Tramway would eventually take over Denver City Cable lines and convert them to electric streetcars.

(facing page) The Tramway's electric cars dominate the scene on Lawrence at 16th. The tall structure next to the building with the "THE AMERICAN" sign is the People's Bank building. Continuing along the right side of the photo, across 16th is the Daniels & Fisher Dry Goods store, the Markham Hotel at 17th (with the tower) and just visible above the roof of Car 131, the Clayton Building, across 17th from the hotel. All of the buildings in this scene were demolished in the late 1960s and early 1970s during Denver's "urban removal" days. *(both, Colorado Historical Society)*

KISTLER
THE STANDARD
THE AMERICAN

IT'S WHAT'S UP FRONT THAT COUNTS

The appendage that appeared on the front of most streetcars has always remained a curiosity, especially as to what to call it. Some say it is a "cow catcher," others a "people catcher" or "fender." It looked like a wooden scoop to a few. They were developed by A.L. Lawton, manager of the Colorado Springs Railway, and applied to all of Denver's cars. In 1899 the company commented that it was well pleased with them. "These fenders have picked up a number of persons, as well as dogs, bicycles, and in one instance, a horse."

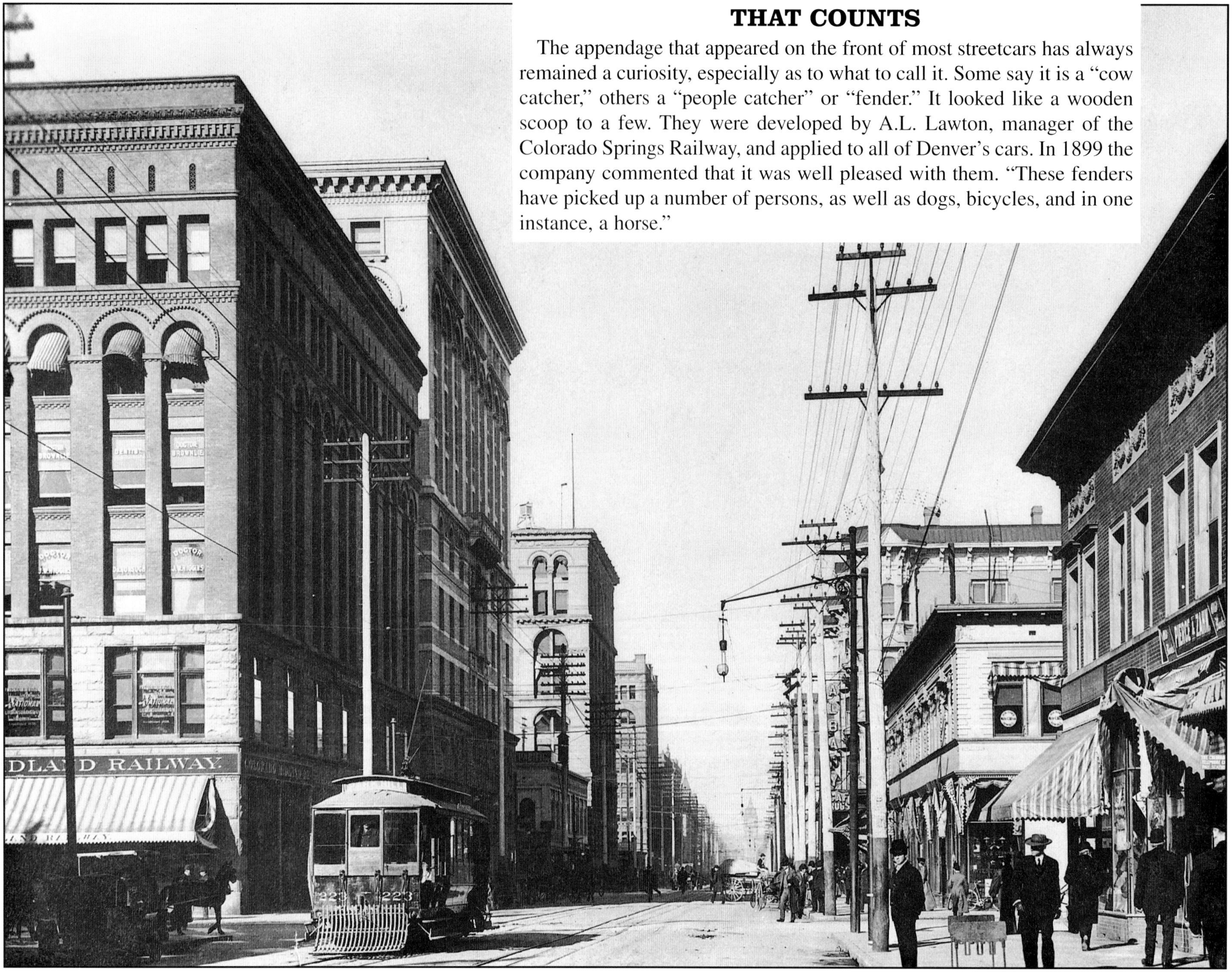

(facing page) Car 223, headed southeast on 17th Street, crosses California. To the immediate left is the California Building, where Colorado Midland Railway had offices. Progressing down that side of the street, the four tall structures are the Equitable, First National Bank, Boston and Ernest & Cranmer buildings. *(Colorado Historical Society)*

(above) Car 383 is going southeast on 18th at California, passing the William Penn Hotel. The hotel, later renamed the Roosevelt, was closed and demolished about 1970 and replaced by a high-rise office building. *(Denver Public Library Western History Department)*

"SEEING DENVER"

OBSERVATION CARS

Operated Every Day in the Year

Sight-Seeing & Educational
Trolly trips around beautiful Denver

An EXPERT GUIDE
ON EVERY CAR

Tickets Fifty Cents

CHILDREN CHARGED FULL FARE

EACH TRIP 25 MILES
EACH TRIP 2 HOURS

ALL AROUND THE TOWN

As an added attraction, and to garner extra revenue, the Tramway company instituted special "Seeing Denver" open-air excursion cars in 1897. A ticket office was located in the Brown Palace Hotel at the corner of 17th and Tremont. Tours from one hour to half a day showed riders the sights of the city. Half and full day trips were provided on a "Wishbone Route" to Golden and Leyden using the narrow gauge lines. Real estate agents realized the opportunity to use the excursions as a tool to show prospective buyers their available properties. *(Colorado Historical Society)*

CURTAINS

The scene is on 15th Street at Cleveland Place in the year 1910. Car 54 passes by as a crowd gathers to watch the demolition of the Metropolitan Theater. The structure was built in 1889 of granite masonry and could seat about 1,000 people. Its construction methods became suspect by city authorities (an inordinate amount of wood comprised the superstructure) but managed to pass inspection. On the night of June 10, 1892, fire broke out, and the conflagration left nothing but the granite walls. A writer of the time stated, "Its destruction was a far more brilliant spectacle than anything ever presented on its stage." The corner is now occupied by a part of the Adam's Mark Hotel complex.

In the background is the Arapahoe County Courthouse which was built in 1883. A fourth floor was added in 1893, and the building was demolished in 1935. The entire block was occupied by the May D&F department store from 1958 until 1993.

Car 54's fate proved more amicable, for its body was preserved and can be dined in at Denver City Cable Railway's powerhouse at 18th and Lawrence, now the Old Spaghetti Factory restaurant. *(Denver Public Library Western History Department)*

AT THE CENTER OF IT ALL

With increased growth of the street railway system, the Tramway felt it prudent to congregate its various departments under one roof. Since all but a few car lines radiated from the business district, it was also wise to locate a carhouse in the heart of the city. As a result, the company decided to erect a two-story carhouse and an eight-story office building at the corner of Arapahoe and 14th streets, less than one block from the Interurban Loop and the Central Loop.

The architects were W.E. and A.A. Fisher, consulting engineers were Crocker and Ketchum and the general contractor was the Whitney-Steen Company. Construction began in March 1910, and the building was ready for occupancy in May 1911.

The two-story carhouse accommodated 63 cars on the lower floor and 48 on the second. The second floor was only for car storage, while each track on the first floor was provided with an inspection pit 291 feet long. A partial third floor, above the carhouse, contained an auditorium with 500 seats, a gymnasium, showers, lockers, reading room, barber shop and bowling alleys—all for the use of employees.

The eight-story administration building's exterior was finished in a rich red "Blackstone" brick laid with wide joints of black mortar and trimmed in ornamental white terra-cotta. The public hall's floors were a light pink Tennessee marble with four-foot high wainscoting in veined white Arizona marble with a base of green Vermont marble.

The first floor had offices for the superintendent of transportation, the treasurer, a lost and found department and a large bulletin room for

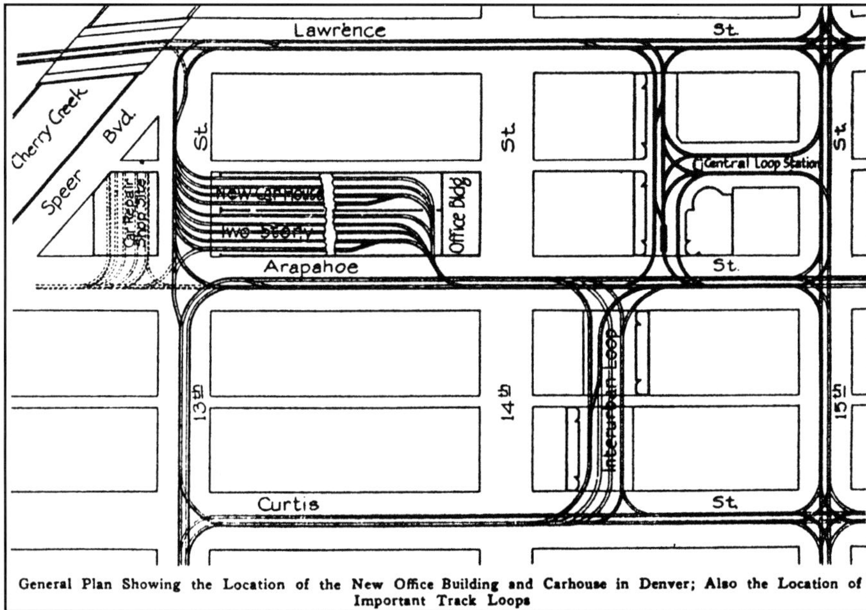

General Plan Showing the Location of the New Office Building and Carhouse in Denver; Also the Location of Important Track Loops

trainmen. The second floor was occupied by physicians, the Tramway Mutual Aid Society and the legal and claim departments. The third, fourth and fifth floors were to be rented out until such time as needed by the company. The auditing department occupied the sixth floor, and the engineering department was on the seventh. The eighth floor was occupied by the president, directors, vice-president and general manager, and the purchasing department.

The Tramway occupied the site until 1956. It was sold in 1973 to the University of Colorado which maintained classrooms and offices in the tower until 1988, when it was vacated. The carhouse has since

(opposite) It is May 1911, and the office tower and carhouse have just been completed. Today the tower is vacant, but the site is listed in the National Register of Historic Places. *(L.C. McClure photo, Colorado Historical Society)*

128. PHOTO. BY CE McCLURE.

MODERN
SCHOOL OF
BUSINESS
5th FLOOR
A. M. KEARNS
ERIFF'S SALE
SIGNS
F. D. STORM'S STUDIO.
MADAME BORDEAUX
CLAIRVOYANT
Dean
Gillespie
SIGN
CO
SIGNS
GEM THEATRE
GREEN RIBBON WHISKY
BAKERY AND LUNCH ROOM
FAMOUS
BAR
CIGARS
920

15TH STREET

(opposite) There was a time when 15th Street was a mix of financial, commercial and entertainment establishments. This view, looking northwest from Champa along the southwest side of the street, shows a multiplicity of small businesses vying for trade. The clothing store in the left foreground is closing and is having a "Sheriff's Sale." Two doors down another business is shuttered, which places the time of this photo to be about 1905. (The Gas and Electric Building will be constructed on the site of this two-story row in 1910.) A few establishments were still open: a bakery and lunch room, the Gem Theatre and a saloon advertising Green Ribbon Whiskey. Second floor tenants include the Dean Gillespie Sign Company, F.D. Storn's Studio, a jewelry shop and Madame Bordeaux—Clairvoyant. On the fourth floor of the Charles Building (completed in 1889) window washers are at work. In later years this building succumbed to a major fire and eventually was replaced by a telephone company building. Up the street at Arapahoe stands the Mining Exchange Building, which opened in 1891. It was demolished in 1963 and replaced by Brooks Towers.

A few years later the scene at 15th and Curtis has changed. Automobiles line the street, the building on the immediate left has replaced a previous structure and, across Arapahoe Street from the Mining Exchange, the Central Bank (1911) has been added to the skyline. All of the structures in this scene are now photographic history. Currently, Brooks Towers occupies the area on the southwest side of 15th, from Curtis to Arapahoe, and the block the bank was on is now a parking lot. *(both, Denver Public Library Western History Department)*

BAKER BROS. MFG. CO.
MASCOT HOUSE LODGING.
Shaw's
Malt.

15TH STREET (continued)

(opposite) Delivery wagons abound in this photo taken at the intersection of 15th and Market. The building at the far left edge of the picture was originally the Tappan Building (built 1867), and the portion nearest the corner (with the three arches on the ground floor) began as a two-story structure in which the Holladay Overland Mail Stage and Express Company was located. A third story was added at a later date to conform with the Tappan Building. The structure still stands but has had its two top stories removed. Across the street and down the block at Blake is the four-story Studebaker Brothers Building. In 1994 it was converted into apartments with retail shops located on the first floor. Barely visible down the street from the Studebaker is the mansard-roofed First National Bank, which stood until 1977 when it was razed following a fire. The steeple of the Asbury United Methodist Church, a Highland landmark to this day, appears in the distance. *(Denver Public Library Western History Department)*

(right) We are looking southeast on 15th Street from Platte. Conspicuous on the right, just beyond the pole with the car stop sign, is a "lock-up box." These were used by Denver's finest to temporarily detain persons who had had too much to drink. Across the street is the Highland Saloon. In later years the building had its second story removed and in 1969 became the popular My Brother's Bar. In the distance a couple of streetcars cross the Platte River on the old 15th Street Bridge. *(Colorado Historical Society)*

AT THE CORNER OF 17TH AND BROADWAY

This view of 17th and Broadway dates from about 1900. Although the Brown Palace Hotel appears on the far left, domestic life remains the order of the day. Coal and ash bins line the alley, with only the steeple of the Central Presbyterian Church interrupting the skyline. Looking east up 17th Avenue, an electric streetcar is just cresting the hill at Grant on its eastbound trip, as a westbound car approaches Broadway.

(facing page) Looking north in about 1905, the intersection has taken on a cosmopolitan appearance. The streetcar remains a part of the picture, but domestic architecture has been all but replaced.

For over a hundred years the Brown Palace Hotel (center left) has anchored the crossroads of 17th and Broadway. Designed by Frank E. Edbrooke, it opened in August 1892 and continues to be the place "Where the world registers." In the distance, the spire of Trinity Methodist Church, designed by Robert Roeschlaub and opened in 1887, pierces the skyline at 18th Avenue.

Another Edbrooke building appears in this photo. The Metropole Hotel, built 1889-90, also contained the Broadway Theater as an integral part of its structure. The 1,620-seat theater was later converted to show motion pictures. Catercorner from the Brown is the Savoy Hotel which opened in 1904.

A combination of changing economics and Denver's high-rise office construction has had a marked impact on this scene. Only the Brown Palace and Trinity Church remain standing. All other structures are now part of the pictorial past. *(both, Denver Public Library Western History Department)*

HOTEL
METROPOLE
AMERICAN & EUROPEAN PLAN
ABSOLUTELY
FIRE PROOF
210. NORTH ON BROADWAY DENVER COLO.
PHOTO. BY C. McCLURE.

SEASON'S GREETINGS ON 16TH STREET

(left) A pattern of shadows dapples 16th Street, created by the trees around the Arapahoe County Court House. Benches are crowded with folks taking advantage of another pleasant summer day in downtown Denver. Tramway car 373 is heading northwest crossing Tremont.

(right) 16th Street is decorated for an Elk's convention as passengers alight from an eastbound Route 23 car at Champa into what appears to be the start of a growing snowstorm. Someone has been diligent enough to cover the radiator of his car with a blanket to protect its contents from freezing. On a day like this, the benches along side the courthouse are more likely crowded with mounting snow flakes then with anything or anyone else! *(both, Colorado Historical Society)*

LET IT SNOW

LET IT SNOW

LET IT SNOW

The blizzard of December 1913 has disabled this eastbound streetcar on 16th Street at Welton. The effect of the accumulated "white stuff" over the front of the car gives it the appearance of a Veronica Lake hair style. The tower of Daniels & Fisher store is vaguely discernible in the background, just left of center. *(Denver Public Library Western History Department)*

OH, THE WEATHER OUTSIDE IS FRIGHTFUL

Known as the "Storm of the Century" the blizzard of December 1913, which produced 47.6 inches of snow, was one of only two occasions that completely disabled streetcar service in Denver.

Snow began falling early Monday morning, December 1st, and except for a short lull on Tuesday, continued to fall until noon on Friday. By Thursday, the Tramway was completely routed in its efforts to keep the lines open and the first complete tie-up in the history of the company occurred. The accompanying photos graphically depict the situation.

(above) Car 111 and a companion are marooned on 17th Avenue, westbound at Lincoln.

(right) Looking down 17th toward Broadway, a line of cars has become disabled by the snow. *(both, Colorado Historical Society)*

(left) Three cars appear to be huddled together for protection against the blizzard. *(Denver Public Library Western History Department)*

(below) The snow has piled up into huge drifts, blocking all progress of the streetcars on Court Place. *(Colorado Historical Society)*

The brunt of the storm came on Thursday, December 4th, accompanied by strong winds that piled the snow into ten-foot drifts. Hotels and rooming houses were jammed by stranded office workers as the streetcars became stalled in their tracks.

BY THE NUMBERS

Car 343 pauses at the end of the Stockyards line, next to the Drover's National Bank. The Route 66 number box is a prominent feature along with the ever-present dash sign. *(Gene McKeever collection)*

BY THE NUMBERS

Beginning in 1916 the Tramway introduced numbered routes. Until that time, all routes had the terminus or route name appearing in the front clerestory. After considering several options, an opaque sign of double-faced sheetmetal with a dark background was selected. The frame was mounted on the front right-hand corner of the roof, with a lamp mounted on each side. Visibility angles were determined so that the number would be plainly seen from either side, as the car approached, until it was nearly opposite a person standing on the curb.

As the fleet was converted to one-man operation, beginning in 1924, the roof mounted numbers began to be replaced with numbers appearing in the upper portion of the right front window. The job was never completely finished for roof-mounted signs remained on four or five cars that were used during rush hour periods until the system was abandoned.

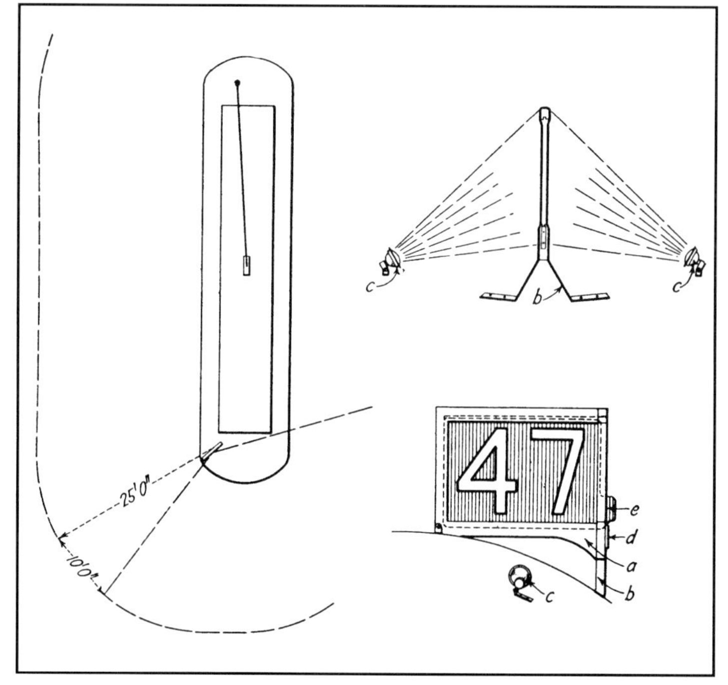

Car 332 sits at the end of the University Park line, Route 8, at Evans and Milwaukee. Typical of the neighborhood was the Evans Store on the northeast corner of the intersection. Built in 1890 by Watson Wesley and Sarah Evans, it was a general store and post office, with Mrs. Evans serving as postmistress until her death in 1934. The car line was abandoned in 1949, but the store continued to be a local gathering spot and grocery store until it closed in 1968. The building remains and has been remodeled into offices. *(Denver Public Library Western History Department)*

HI HO SILVER!

From the start of horsecar service the application of different colors on the cars became an important factor in identifying the various companys' equipment that provided service in the Mile High City. After consolidation, and continuing until 1925, a general paint scheme was developed that used a striking combination of "Amaranth Red" on the main panel of the cars along with "Car Body Yellow" on the lower panels and upper framework. (*see front cover*)

During a campaign, prior to a May 1925 referendum to allow Denver Tramway to introduce supplemental bus service, the company introduced a silver painted streetcar, No. 831. The lettering, car wheels and all steel work were black. Running among all the red cars, it created much interest.

The *Denver Post* explained the innovation by stating that H.H. Tammen, one of the owners of the paper, approached Ernest Stenger of the Tramway and said, "Colonel Stenger, I've seen red streetcars, green ones, yellow ones, and black ones, but I've never seen a silver streetcar. Why don't you paint all the Denver cars silver, so that you'll have something no other street railway system has? It will attract attention and cause comment, and soon people all over the country will know of Denver as the city of silver streetcars."

An 800 series car, resplendent in its silver paint scheme, has stopped at Cleveland Place on 16th Street. To the right is the Majestic Building, and the circular pedestrian island occupies the triangle formed by 16th, Cleveland Place and Broadway. *(Denver Tramway photo, E.J. Haley collection)*

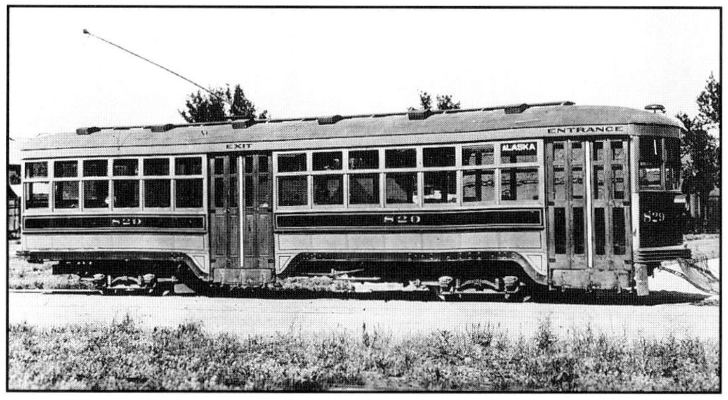

BEFORE

Before silver was applied, the Tramway paint scheme was "Amaranth Red" on the main panel and "Car Body Yellow" on the lower panels and upper framework.

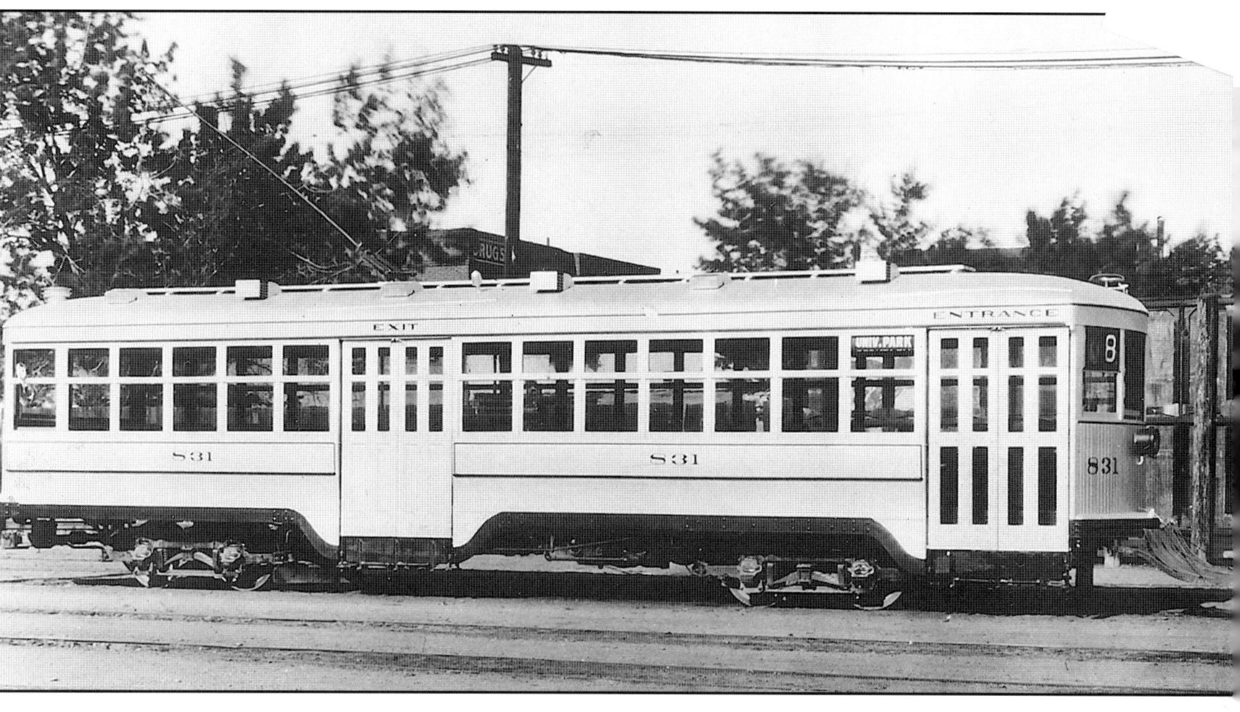

SILVERWARE

The first to receive what became the experimental silver paint scheme was car 831. Reports of the time suggest that the trim was black, although some say it was dark green. Fifty 800 series cars were built by the Tramway in 1922-1925 and were the last constructed for the system. *(three photos, Gene McKeever collection)*

AFTER

After experiencing problems with the silver paint "Chrome Yellow" was selected and became the standard until streetcars were abandoned.

As a result of Tammen's suggestion the company painted about 50 of its cars with an aluminum paint, a flat silver hue. In an industry publication of the period, it was stated that the cars were "pretty," but as they rounded a curve with the sun shining on them, they glistened with such splendor that automobile drivers and pedestrians were blinded by the reflection. The company also found that the unvarnished silver color was hard to keep clean. After only a year had gone by, the aluminum paint scheme was scuttled and a semi-varnished chrome yellow was selected as the standard for all 370 cars. This would remain the color of the fleet until the demise of the cars.

A SIGN OF THE TIMES

In 1926, *Electric Railway Journal* reported the following:

> As he stood at the "Loop" and watched the various cars wind around, a representative of the *Journal* smiled his approval when he saw on the front dashboard a large sign which read:
>
> ***BUY A HOME IN DENVER***
> ***It's a Great Place to Live***

Upon investigating who was responsible for the prideful advertising he found that it was suggested by the purchasing agent of the company, W.G. Simmonds. He reported that "the directors took to it like a duck does to water."

Tramway Vice-President Robertson stated that it was the company's duty to do anything it could to build up its already beautiful city. "We shall carry these signs for an indefinite period. There are more than a hundred slogans. We expect to change the cards twice a week, and it may be that we will vary the exhibit."

The article went on to say:

> Summing it all up one is forced to conclude that the Tramway is doing for the city more than any other method, hence various improvement associations, the realtors, the city fathers are calling in person, via the telephone and by the use of the mails to say to President Stenger and Vice-President Robertson, "Oh boy, but you folks have hit upon a wonderful educative idea. Our sincere thanks, appreciation and obligations are yours. As advertisers you may go to the head of the class."

One man upon leaving Mr. Robertson said, "Never again will I accuse you folks of being nickel nursers."

(facing page) One of the Tramway's dashboard signs is prominently displayed on car 845 as its motorman sits on the car's fender. *(Gene McKeever collection)*

RUSH HOUR ACCOMMODATIONS

(right) The Tramway was noted for providing excellent service to its riders. To take care of rush hour crowds it depended on a fleet of streetcars with trailers. Car 54 and trailer 502 are northbound on Broadway at 14th Avenue. The apartment building is long gone, and the site is now planted with grass and trees in front of Denver's main library. *(Colorado Historical Society)*

Below, a southbound Route 5 car and trailer hasten down Broadway. The Hotel Yale was at 1047 Broadway; the building is still in existence today. *(Denver Public Library Western History Department)*

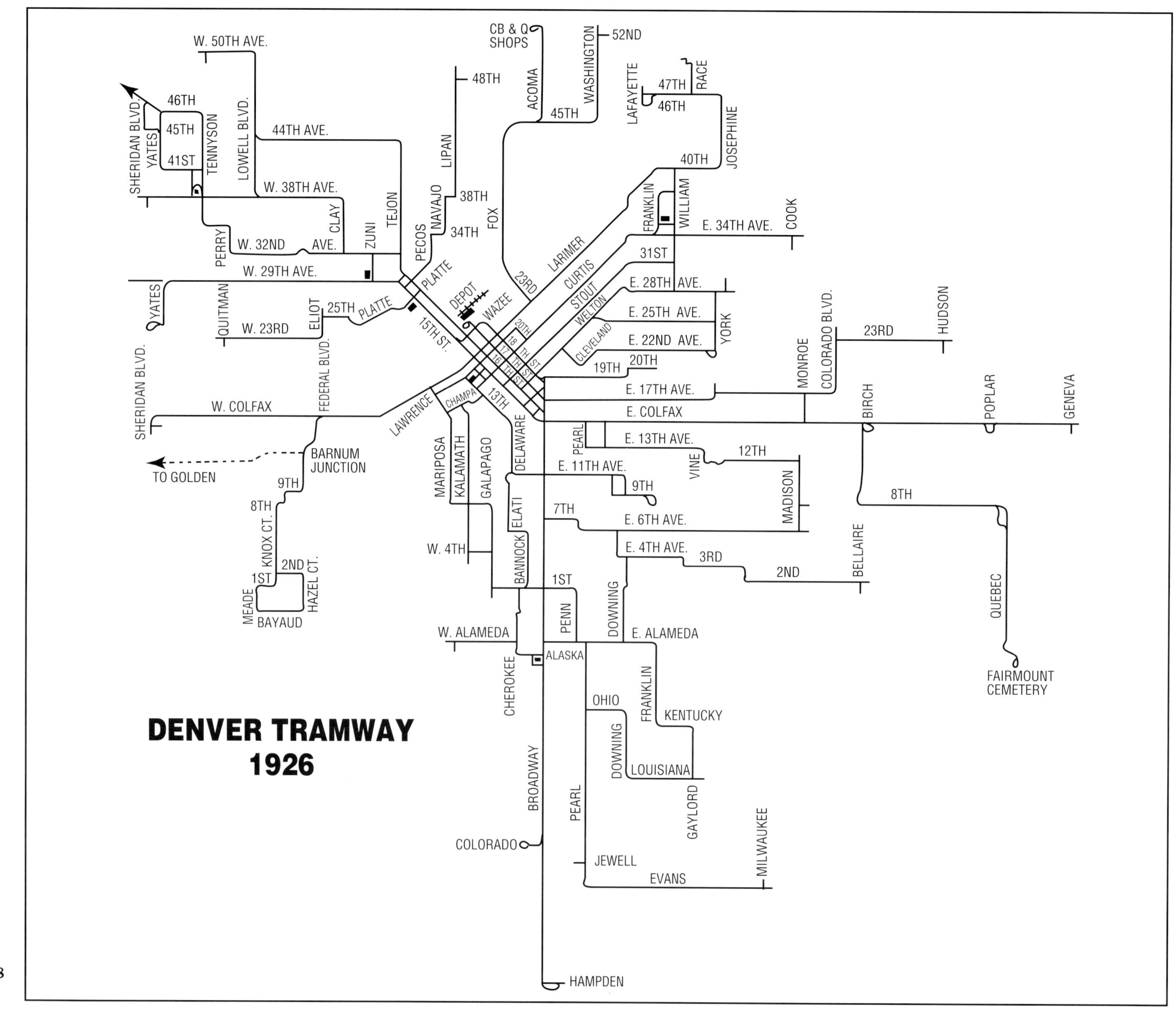
DENVER TRAMWAY
1926
W. 50TH AVE.
46TH
45TH
41ST
SHERIDAN BLVD.
YATES
TENNYSON
LOWELL BLVD.
44TH AVE.
W. 38TH AVE.
CLAY
W. 32ND
AVE.
PERRY
W. 29TH AVE.
YATES
QUITMAN
W. 23RD
ELIOT
25TH
PLATTE
ZUNI
TEJON
PECOS
NAVAJO
LIPAN
48TH
38TH
34TH
FOX
PLATTE
15TH ST.
DEPOT
WAZEE
CB & Q
SHOPS
ACOMA
45TH
WASHINGTON
52ND
23RD
LARIMER
CURTIS
STOUT
WELTON
CLEVELAND
LAFAYETTE
47TH
46TH
RACE
JOSEPHINE
40TH
FRANKLIN
WILLIAM
E. 34TH AVE.
COOK
31ST
E. 28TH
AVE.
E. 25TH AVE.
E. 22ND AVE.
YORK
19TH
20TH
E. 17TH AVE.
MONROE
COLORADO BLVD.
23RD
HUDSON
E. COLFAX
BIRCH
POPLAR
GENEVA
SHERIDAN BLVD.
W. COLFAX
FEDERAL BLVD.
LAWRENCE
CHAMPA
13TH
BARNUM
JUNCTION
TO GOLDEN
9TH
8TH
KNOX CT.
2ND
1ST
HAZEL CT.
MEADE
BAYAUD
MARIPOSA
KALAMATH
GALAPAGO
DELAWARE
PEARL
E. 13TH AVE.
12TH
VINE
E. 11TH AVE.
9TH
MADISON
8TH
ELATI
7TH
E. 6TH AVE.
W. 4TH
BANNOCK
E. 4TH AVE.
3RD
2ND
BELLAIRE
QUEBEC
1ST
DOWNING
PENN
W. ALAMEDA
E. ALAMEDA
ALASKA
CHEROKEE
FAIRMOUNT
CEMETERY
OHIO
FRANKLIN
KENTUCKY
DOWNING
LOUISIANA
GAYLORD
BROADWAY
PEARL
MILWAUKEE
COLORADO
JEWELL
EVANS
HAMPDEN

BEYOND THE LIMITS

Car .05 skirts Coors Brewery as it makes its way into downtown Golden. *(Gene McKeever collection)*

(above) Originally standard gauge, the line to Globeville, which terminated at 52nd and Washington, was changed to 42-inch gauge in 1921. It succumbed to buses in 1928. *(Denver Public Library Western History Department)*

At left, car 331 is at the end of the line in Aurora at East Colfax and Geneva. Streetcar service was provided to this point until 1932. *(Colorado Historical Society)*

Over the years, 16th Street became Denver's retail shopping street. Along its length from Broadway to Larimer one could find a few of the larger motion picture houses (Denver, Paramount, Tabor), retail establishments (Denver Dry Goods, May Company, Neusteter, J.C. Penney, W.T. Grant, Kress, Woolworth, Joslin's, Daniels & Fisher) and various other businesses. The above scene, looking northwest from Glenarm and taken on October 13, 1933, graphically represents the amount of activity that was once found along the street. In June 1940, the Tramway abandoned a number of car lines and moved the remaining ones off 16th, between Larimer and Broadway, to 15th and 17th. Today, the street is a mall, the movie theatres and large retail stores are gone and the entire block on the left is a parking lot. *(Gene McKeever collection)*

AND THE DAYS DWINDLED DOWN TO A PRECIOUS FEW

The "Roaring Twenties" would see the Tramway at its finest. Except for a bitter strike by operating personnel in August 1920, that would culminate in the second and only other total shut down of the system, the riding public could rely on a streetcar system that was second to none in the industry. With a total of over 260 miles of city trackage the Tramway had one mile of track for every 1,000 people in Denver. This compared with a national average of only a half mile per 1,000 population served. By the mid-1920s the company had constructed 50 new cars (the last to be built for Denver) and added them to the fleet.

But the "love affair" with the streetcar proved fleeting as the public discovered a new love, the automobile, and abandoned its faithful friend in growing numbers. The economic hardship of the 1930s, the expanding network of modern highways and an afFORDable car in every garage would begin to unravel the twin ribbons of steel.

Saved from total abandonment by the country's entrance into the Second World War, with its attendant shortage of necessary commodities, streetcars were once again called upon to provide yeoman service that the public would take for granted.

The public's renewed dependency on the streetcar would prove to be short lived. In less then ten years, by the late 1940s, the precipitous drop in ridership would prove fatal. The private lines of the Tramway were no longer able to compete with the public roads of the community. By mid-1950 the wires came down, the tracks were torn up or covered over, and the yellow cars scrapped. The future would roll on rubber tires, over increasing ribbons of concrete, with growing brown clouds of pollution obscuring the horizon. Such is "progress"!

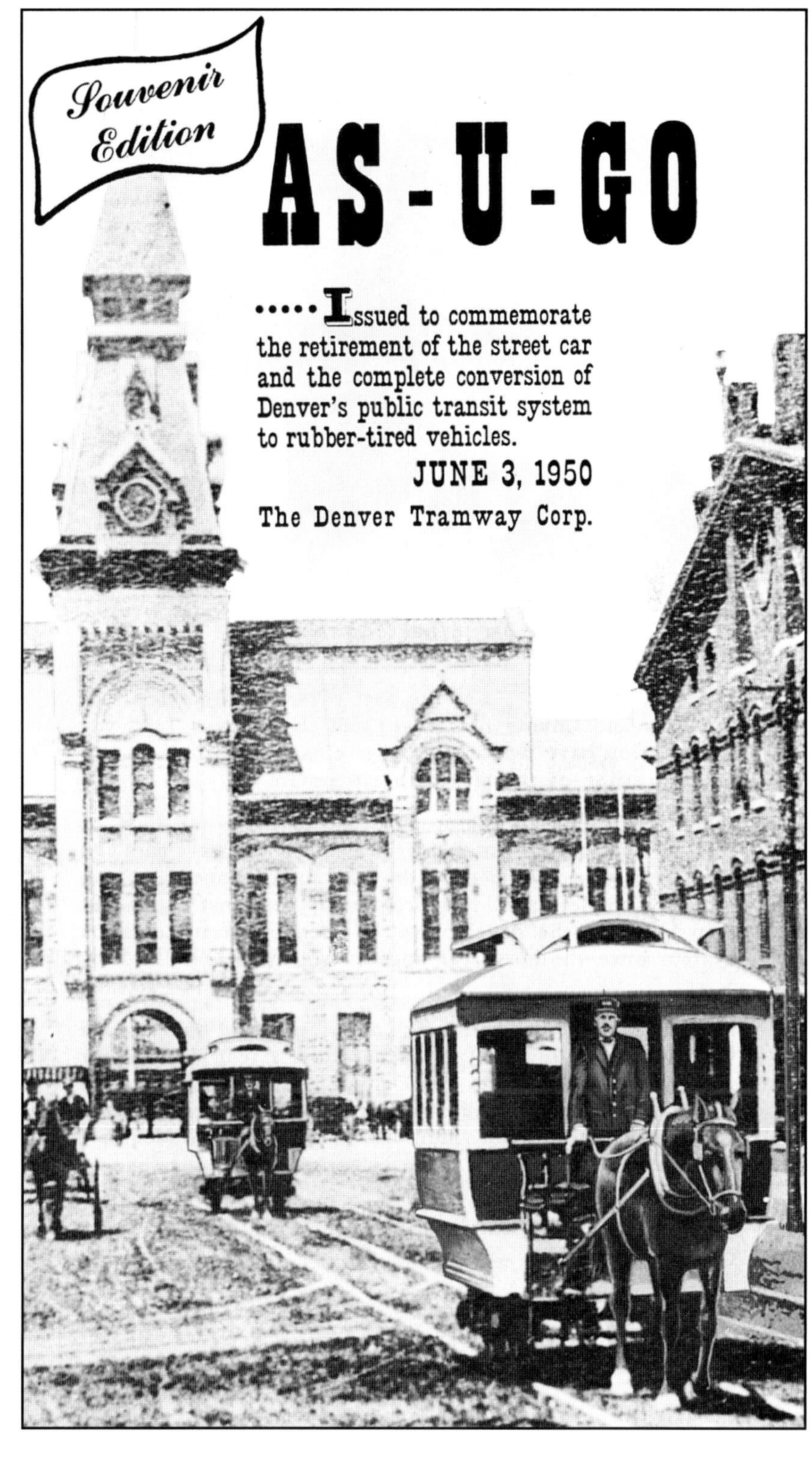

During the last few weeks of city streetcar service the Tramway provided a souvenir edition of AS-U-GO to commemorate the end of an era. *(author's collection)*

THOSE CURIOUS DECIMALS

For many years the decimals that appeared on certain of the Tramway streetcars remained a mystery. A series of cars was given decimal fleet numbers, .01 through .07, but the reason remained lost in a fog until recently. The unusual numbering system was used by the Tramway to designate the equipment assigned to subsidiary Denver & Northwestern for the three-foot six-inch gauge suburban lines to Golden, Arvada and Leyden. The curious numbers remained on the cars until the final demise of the system on July 2, 1950. Denver's electric fractions were unique in the streetcar world.

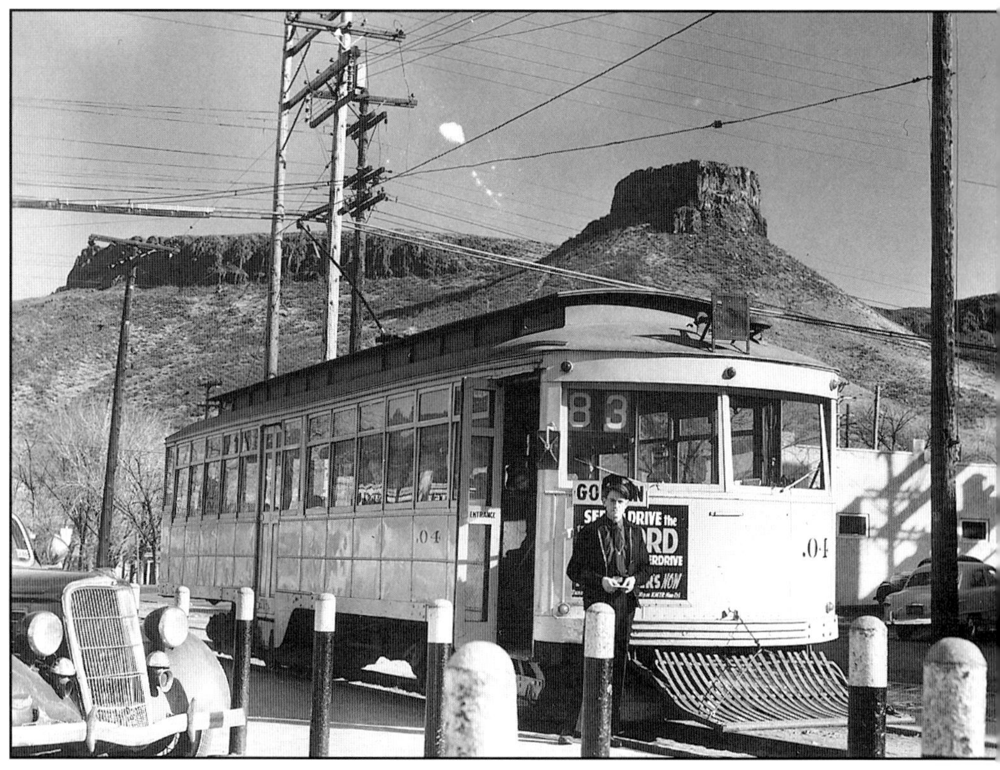

(above) Car .04 rests at the end of Route 83 in Golden. The plethora of wires that frame Castle Rock supply electricity and telephone service to the community and are not connected with the trolley.

(left) A motorman stands beside car .03 near the end of Route 82 at the Leyden coal mines. The dual gauge track was used by the Tramway so that standard gauge gondolas could be hauled from the mines to railroads at Leyden and Arvada junctions. *(both, David K. Clint, Jr. photos, Gene McKeever collection)*

TO THE END OF THE LINE

Car 840 has just turned from 17th Street and dropped a few passengers off in front of Union Station. It will continue on Wynkoop to a loop that was located next to the 16th Street Viaduct. Route 6 was abandoned in November 1948, but all structures in this photo remain standing.

(above) Car 29 sits on the wye of Route 64 at East 34th Avenue and Cook. This line was abandoned in September 1949.

(left) Car 842 is at the end of Route 5 at South Gaylord and Louisiana. One of the last lines to operate in the city, it was abandoned on June 3, 1950. *(all, Gene McKeever collection)*

Car 126, built by the Woeber Carriage Company in 1911, turns from Arapahoe onto 15th Street after making a circuit of the Central Loop, the entrance to which is a half a block on the left, to the rear of the car. None of the buildings in this scene are still with us, and Elitch's closed its amusement park in north Denver in 1994 and moved to a new site in the Platte River valley. *(B.H. Ward photo, Museum collection)*

Today the street is paved, the Hudson and other automobiles are now collector's items and the streetcar disappeared from the scene in 1950, but all the buildings remain at the intersection of West 32nd Avenue and Zuni in north Denver. Car 839, pictured on May 13, 1949, was among the last series of cars built by the Tramway during 1922-1925. *(Tom Gray photo, Don Robertson collection)*

IN MEMORY OF A FINE PHOTOGRAPHER

During the 1940s, and until the Tramway's car lines were abandoned, David K. Clint, Jr., was out photographing the system. I never knew Dave but when I came across his work in the collection of Gene McKeever, I could not resist including a selection of his photos in this book. Killed in a tragic accident, his work remains as a record of his fine craftsmanship. The following pages attest to his keen eye for composition.

Car 70 has just pulled off 15th Street and entered Central Loop to board a group of passengers for Route 75 to Barnum. By the looks of it, it is another nice spring day in Denver. Elitch's Gardens is advertising the citywide YMCA Boy's Spring Party to be held at the amusement park on June 4th. Route 75 was abandoned in September 1949, and the site of the loop is now a parking lot.

As a cost cutting measure in 1932, the Tramway discontinued the portion of the East Colfax line from Poplar to Geneva streets in Aurora. A large, brick passenger shelter served the loop at Poplar where we see car 804 preparing to make its return trip to downtown. Route 14, along with the short turn Route 10 that looped at Birch and Colfax, remained in service until the end, June 3, 1950. *(two photos, David K. Clint, Jr., Gene McKeever collection)*

What a difference a day can make! According to the clock on the Lantz Dry Cleaning billboard, it is 5:20 on the morning of a slightly blustery, snowy day. No automobiles or pedestrians are in view on East Colfax at Josephine as a lone streetcar heads west toward downtown. It looks like a scene from the movie *On The Beach*.

The front of the car attests to the fact that a wet snow has been falling, but the temperature cannot be far from freezing as puddles of water appear on the street. The motorman has changed the destination sign to read Route 0, as he has ended his day's run and brought 342 to the carhouse. *(two photos, David K. Clint, Jr., Gene McKeever collection)*

The Tramway maintained a fleet of work cars for all weather eventualities. Although a winter storm's accumulation of snow never remained on the ground for very long, the company had to clear its tracks. Sweeper 4 is doing its job in front of the main entrance to Lakeside Park on Sheridan Boulevard.

At the end of most car lines the Tramway placed wooden boxes to store sand. A motorman could transfer the sand into a receptacle on his car, when its supply was getting low. An application of the grit gave extra traction to start or stop a streetcar on rails that were wet or icy. In 1923, the Tramway rebuilt trailer 435 into sand car 763 to deliver the commodity to the boxes. Here workers transfer sand from 763 to the box at South Gaylord and Louisiana. *(two photos, David K. Clint, Jr., Gene McKeever collection)*

The afternoon sun is shining brightly on the side of car 819 as it stops to let off passengers at the Industrial School stop. Car 819 was originally built by the Tramway as a city car but was converted, along with the 818, from 42-inch gauge to standard in March 1924 for use on Route 84 between Denver and Golden.

RUSH TO THE FOOTHILLS

Before electric wires were strung and the sound of electric traction motors was heard in Golden, a standard gauge steam railroad, the Denver Lakewood & Golden, was completed there in 1891. In 1901 the Denver & Northwestern Railway (controlled by Denver City Tramway) constructed a 42-inch gauge electric line to Arvada and Leyden and in March 1904 opened a branch into downtown Golden. In 1909 the standard gauge steam line (by then the Denver & Intermountain Railroad) was purchased by the Tramway and converted to electric operation.

Car 818 pounds across the trestle over Kinney's Run, minutes after leaving the terminus in Golden, enroute to the Interurban Loop in downtown Denver. A 1943 timetable listed close to 20 daily departures each way from Denver and Golden on Route 84. It took under 50 minutes to traverse the 13-mile route, including numerous stops. In 1995 the right-of-way remains in place from Federal Boulevard in Denver to Quail Street in Lakewood. *(two photos, David K. Clint, Jr., Gene McKeever collection)*

Looking north, this low angle view at Arvada Junction catches car .05 on Route 82. The Colorado & Southern Railway bridge is in the foreground with the Grandview Avenue automobile bridge just beyond.

A typical sunny day in Colorado—there are lots of them out here—and a typical scene from the time of the trolley. A few passengers have just alighted from car .05 at the Wadsworth stop, while a young boy (whose head and part of his bike are just visible beyond the cattle guard in the foreground) watches the activity. *(two photos, David K. Clint, Jr., Gene McKeever collection)*

The clickety-clack sound that car .02 was making as it crossed over the rail joints and rushed southbound through Arvada Cut seems almost audible to us in this timeless scene.

Car .05 stops at Olivet to pick up a group of passengers bound for Denver on a balmy day. Most windows are open on the crowded car, giving passengers a chance to enjoy the breeze that will pass through once the .05 is underway. The turnstile in the foreground permitted access to the fenced-in station area and kept out large, four-legged creatures. *(two photos, David K. Clint, Jr., Gene McKeever collection)*

The "Lone Ranger" among the decimal fleet on the 42-inch gauge interurban routes to Golden and Leyden was car 130. It began interurban service shortly after car .07 was destroyed in an accident on March 1, 1942, but never received a decimal number. The camera has captured it on the bridge over Clear Creek.

No, this is not a 1950 Ford! It is interurban .06 on 12th Street, just off Washington in Golden, with a sign on its dash advertising an arch rival. Time was running out for the line as the abandonment date of July 2, 1950, was fast approaching. *(two photos, David K. Clint, Jr., Gene McKeever collection)*

GOODBYE FOREVER!

It is just past midnight on Sunday, June 4, 1950, and Dave Clint has taken this spectacular time exposure from the Mining Exchange Building. Lights from passing automobiles make streaks across the picture, the illuminated dome of the State Capitol appears in the distance, and some of the 13,000 lights on the Gas and Electric Building are visible to the right. Route 14 car 805 stops at the corner of 15th and Curtis just a few blocks from its final destination at Central Loop and its rendezvous with destiny. It will arrive at 12:10 A.M., the last car to use that terminal, as the Tramway completes it conversion of city car lines to buses. *(David K. Clint, Jr. photo, Gene McKeever collection)*

Below is a Denver Tramway Company city fare token, reproduced double its actual size. *(Syd Joseph collection)*

DENVER & INTERURBAN

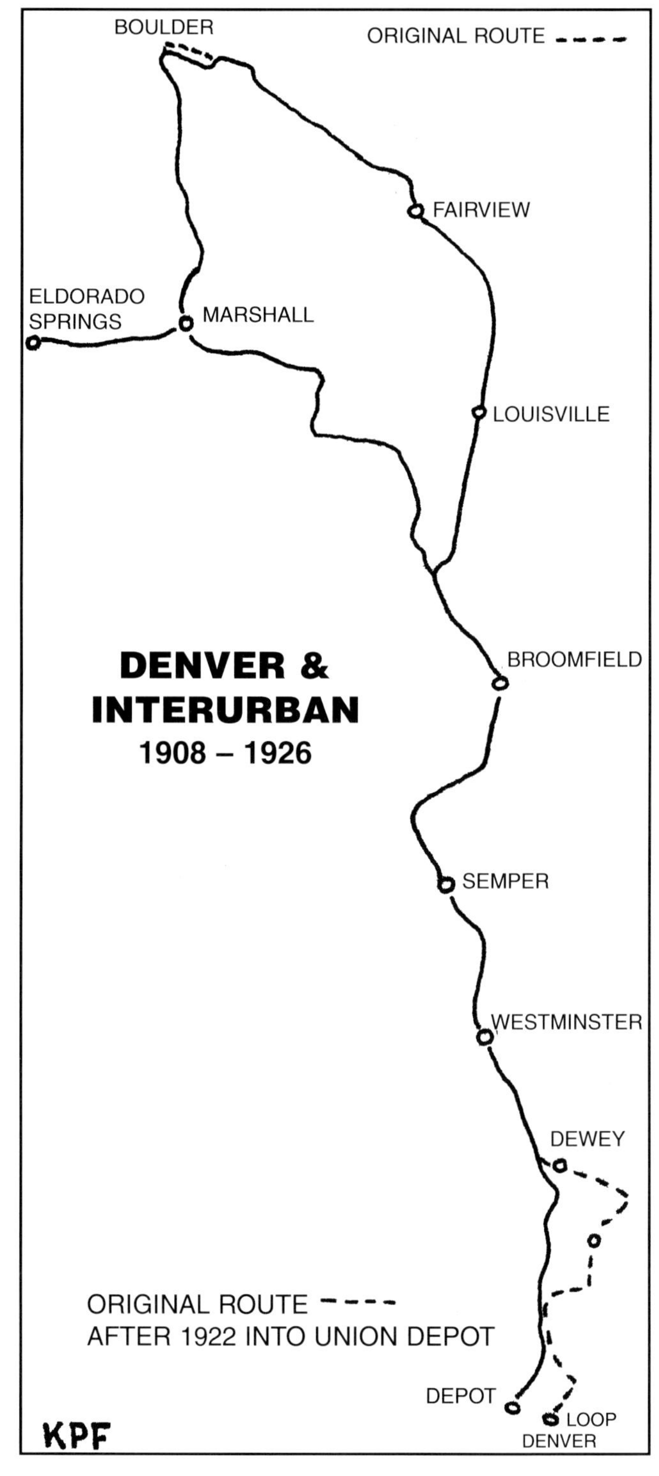

DENVER & INTERURBAN

Built as a wholly-owned subsidiary of the Colorado & Southern Railway, the Denver & Interurban's physical plant was unique in the west. Its standards, other than where it operated over city streets, were first class. The cars were big! St. Louis Car Company completed twelve railroad-sized, 55-foot, steel underframed behemoths that weighed in at 125,000 pounds each. The cars were equipped to operate on 550-volt direct current over the city lines in Denver and Boulder, and on 11,000-volt alternating current in open country.

Originally proposed to connect Denver with Fort Collins (D&I built the city system in Fort Collins, which was intended to provide an entrance into that community) the system was completed between the Mile High City and Boulder on June 23, 1908.

(page 91) A Denver & Interurban car streaks along tangent track near Semper, between Westminster and Broomfield. *(L.C. McClure photo)*

(opposite page) The size of the cars is very apparent as they congregate next to a steam train at the Louisville station. *(Edward Tangen photo)*

(left) A quaint station with a diminutive tower was built at Westminster. *(L.C.McClure photo)*

(below left) This 1919 schedule called for a 75-minute running time, including stops, between Denver & Boulder. *(all, E.J. Haley collection)*

75 MINUTES TO BOULDER IN THE FOOTHILLS

DENVER

Time Tables

ELECTRIC TRAINS

Between

Denver, Louisville, Marshall, Eldorado Springs and Boulder

Corrected to June 1, 1919

Subject to change without notice

The Denver & Interurban R. R.

Wm. H. EDMUNDS, Receiver

TICKET OFFICES

Denver: Interurban Station. Phone Main 990

Boulder: Union Station. Phone Boulder 99

The 51-mile line ran from the Interurban Loop in downtown Denver, over dual gauge Tramway track to Globeville, alongside C&S track to Burns Junction and then on the C&S main track to Boulder via two routes that comprised a loop. One ran via Louisville and the other via Marshall. A branch operated from Marshall to Eldorado Springs.

Because of the sparsely settled area which it served, it was never a financial success. The line was, however, able to improve operations by removing its cars from city streets in both terminal cities. Operation into Union Station in Denver began on September 24, 1922. But receiverships, coupled with one particularly horrendous accident, combined to do the line in. The company ceased operation on December 15, 1926.

Car M-155 has halted in the 1900 block of Broadway in downtown Boulder, next to the company's station. The photo was taken prior to relocation of the track off city streets. *(Carnegie Branch Library for Local History, Boulder Historical Society)*

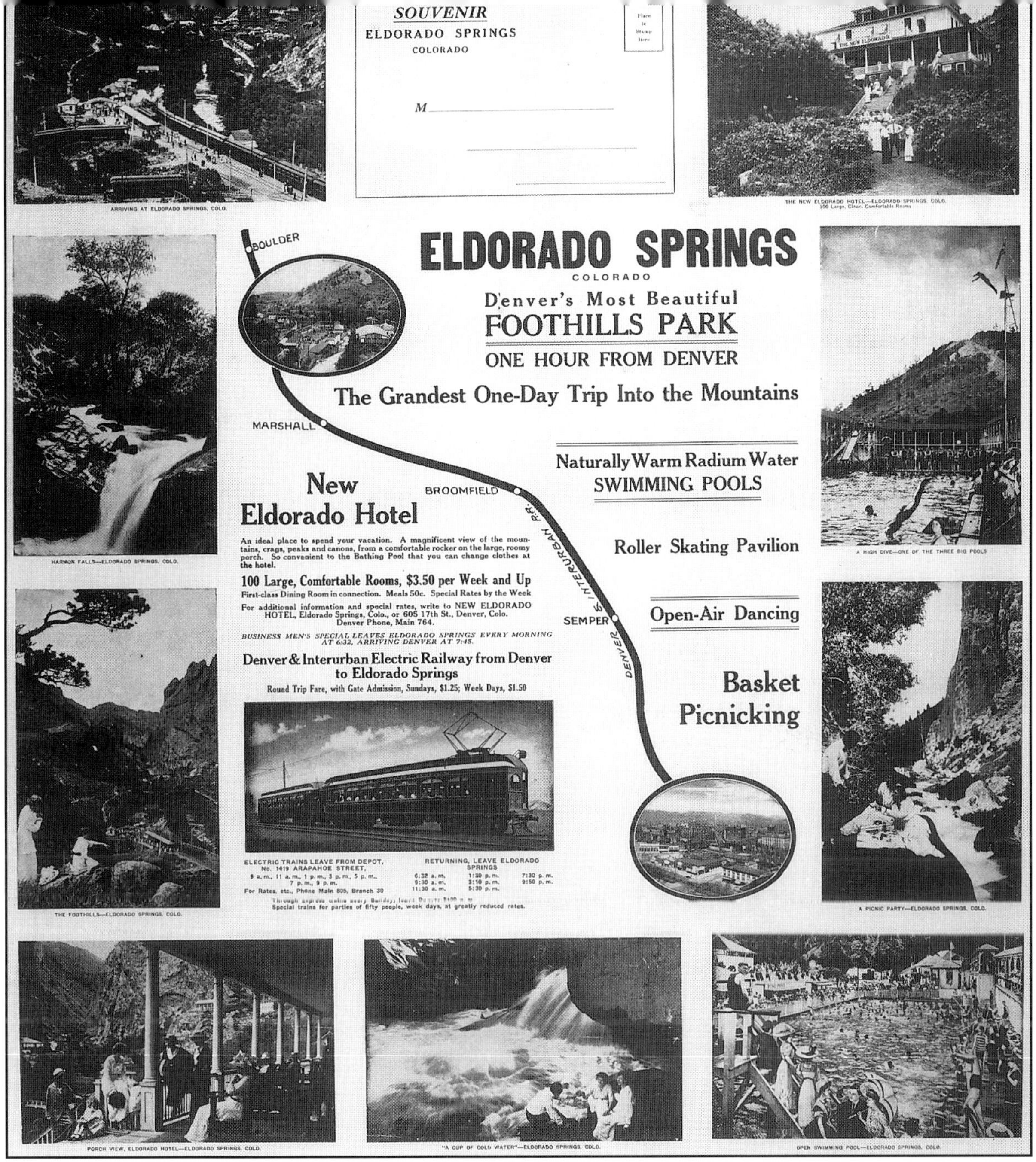
SOUVENIR
ELDORADO SPRINGS
COLORADO
M
ELDORADO SPRINGS
COLORADO
Denver's Most Beautiful
FOOTHILLS PARK
ONE HOUR FROM DENVER
The Grandest One-Day Trip Into the Mountains
BOULDER
MARSHALL
BROOMFIELD
SEMPER
DENVER & INTERURBAN R.R.
New
Eldorado Hotel
An ideal place to spend your vacation. A magnificent view of the mountains, crags, peaks and canons, from a comfortable rocker on the large, roomy porch. So convenient to the Bathing Pool that you can change clothes at the hotel.
100 Large, Comfortable Rooms, $3.50 per Week and Up
First-class Dining Room in connection. Meals 50c. Special Rates by the Week
For additional information and special rates, write to NEW ELDORADO HOTEL, Eldorado Springs, Colo., or 605 17th St., Denver, Colo. Denver Phone, Main 764.
BUSINESS MEN'S SPECIAL LEAVES ELDORADO SPRINGS EVERY MORNING AT 6:32, ARRIVING DENVER AT 7:45.
Denver & Interurban Electric Railway from Denver to Eldorado Springs
Round Trip Fare, with Gate Admission, Sundays, $1.25; Week Days, $1.50
ELECTRIC TRAINS LEAVE FROM DEPOT, No. 1419 ARAPAHOE STREET,
9 a.m., 11 a.m., 1 p.m., 3 p.m., 5 p.m., 7 p.m., 9 p.m.
For Rates, etc., Phone Main 805, Branch 30
RETURNING, LEAVE ELDORADO SPRINGS
6:32 a.m. 9:30 a.m. 11:30 a.m.
1:30 p.m. 3:10 p.m. 5:30 p.m.
7:30 p.m. 9:50 p.m.
Special trains for parties of fifty people, week days, at greatly reduced rates.
Naturally Warm Radium Water
SWIMMING POOLS
Roller Skating Pavilion
Open-Air Dancing
Basket
Picnicking

(above) This souvenir poster, which could be folded up and mailed, was available to guests at Eldorado Springs. *(Carnegie Branch Library for Local History, Boulder)*

(right) A round-trip fare from Denver, plus admission to Eldorado Springs, was $1.25 on Sundays and $1.50 on weekdays. *(author's collection)*

ELDORADO SPRINGS

In South Boulder Canyon local developers started a summer resort in 1904. It featured an outdoor swimming pool, heated by an adjacent hot spring. Realizing that money could be made if the resort was more accessible, they built a three-mile railroad to a connection with the Colorado & Southern at Marshall in 1907. The operation, called the Eldorado Springs Railway, used automobiles running on railroad wheels.

In 1908 a hotel was opened, and the Denver & Interurban purchased and electrified the line in order to bring in guests. The steady, two percent grade from Marshall to Eldorado Springs became the highest point reached by the D & I—6,000 feet above sea level. The area became an immediate hit with as many as 2,000 people arriving on summer weekends. In 1916, two guests were a honeymooning second lieutenant named Dwight D. Eisenhower and his new bride, Mamie.

ISSUED BY
The Denver & Interurban R. R.
ADMISSION COUPON.
ADMIT ONE PERSON
—TO—
Eldorado Springs
AND RETURN.
No.
ISSUED BY
The Denver & Interurban R. R.
William H. Edmunds, Receiver.
ADMISSION COUPON.
ADMIT ONE PERSON
—TO—
Eldorado Springs Resort
Good Three Days including Date Stamped on Back.
Form D I-16
ELDORADO SPRINGS
AND RETURN.
No. B
5929

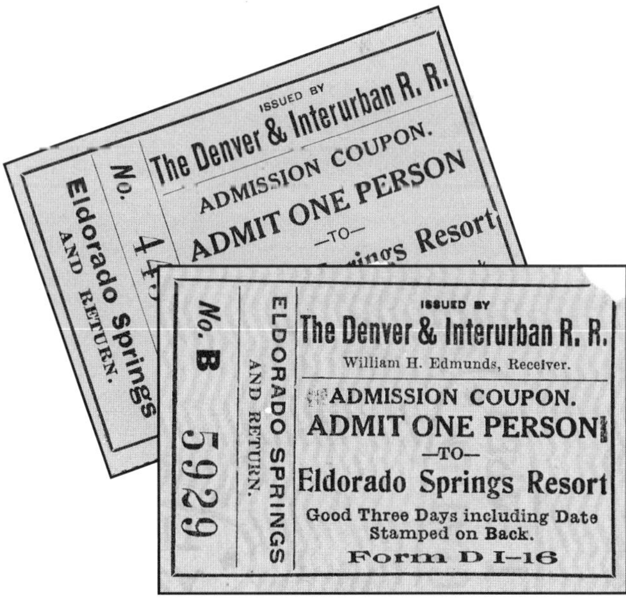

From almost the start of service in Boulder, the Denver & Interurban was anxious to remove its operation from city streets. In 1917, the Boulder City Council finally approved D & I's request to vacate its street operation and begin service over Colorado & Southern tracks to the railroad's depot. Until the 11,000-volt catenary could be erected, steam locomotives brought the cars into the station. In this photo the catenary is up and energized and interurban M-156 has just arrived. *(Carnegie Branch Library for Local History, Boulder Historical collection)*

DURANGO

COLUMBINE
ARPER RYE
CLUB
DURANGO, BROOKSIDE
6
AND ANI AS CITY

DURANGO

Durango was founded by the Denver & Rio Grande Railway in 1880. The town was built not far from Carbon Mountain (called "Walking Mountain" because it was at one time thought to show signs of tumbling headlong into the valley). The first mail was carried in by anyone who happened by, water was hauled from springs and sold for 40 cents a barrel, and court was held in a large room over the general store. Some historic records have stated that the notorious Stockton-Eskridge gang, which carried its warfare throughout the county, one day had an hour-long "shoot-out" with vigilantes on the town's main street.

In 1891-1892, after a temporary lull in its fortunes, Durango boomed once again. In 1891, the Durango Railway & Realty Company built the Main Avenue Railway, a horsecar line. This only ran for a short time because "the crews were abusive and insulting to patrons, and the cars invariably pulled away from the railroad station before all incoming passengers could get aboard."

The Durango Trust purchased the defunct horsecar line in 1892, converted it to electricity and extended it to the Sunnyside Addition. Amazingly it survived the panic of 1893, and its two trolleys continued to run the two miles from the railroad depot in Durango to Animas City. As the years went by the company purchased additional equipment and eventually owned three open and five closed cars.

Better roads and the ubiquitous automobile hastened the demise of one of the smallest street railway systems ever to operate in the United States. A hearing was granted the company by the Public Utilities Commission on September 17, 1920, at which time the owners presented evidence showing that not even operating expenses were being covered. The commission permitted the line to abandon, and all operations came to an end in 1921.

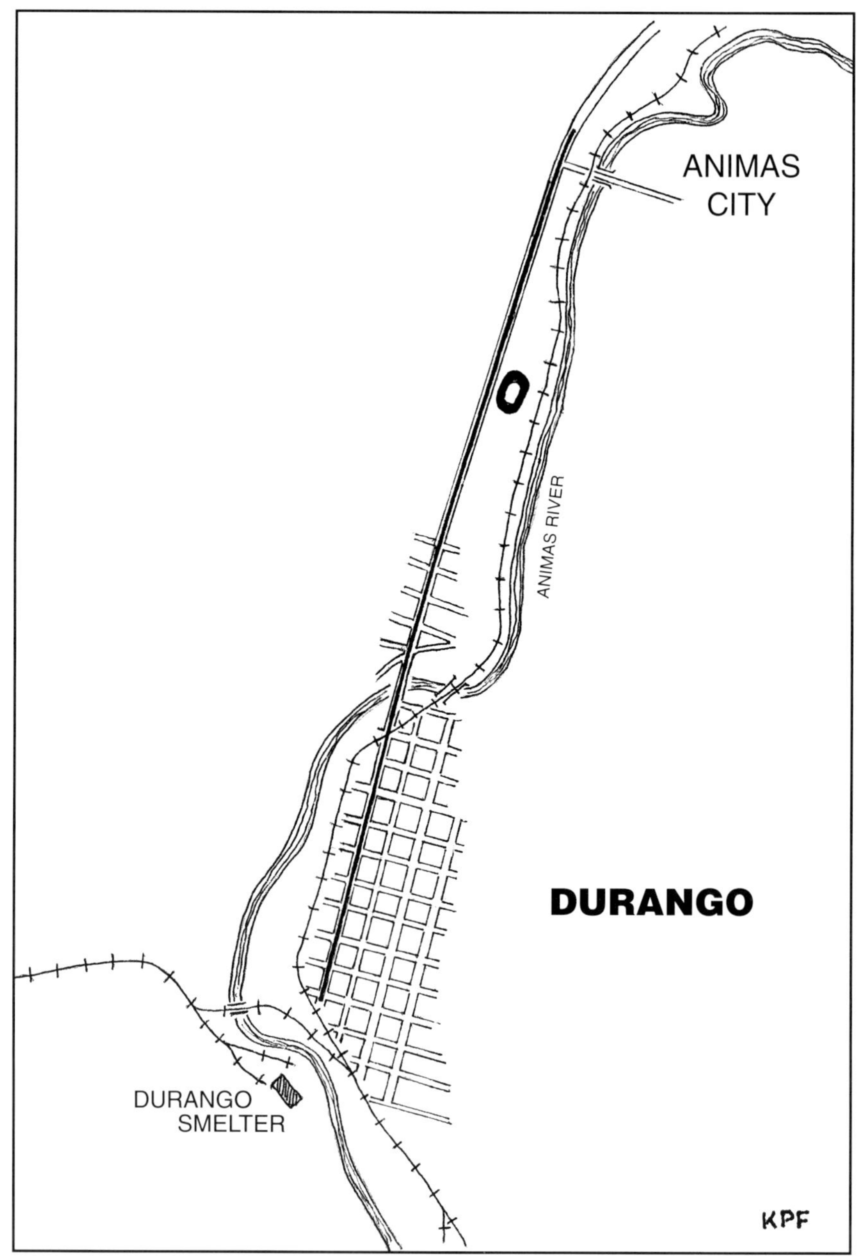

(previous page) Open car 6 proceeds northbound on Main Avenue circa 1916. The script across the dash reads: Durango, Brookside and Animas City. *(George L.Beam photo, E.J. Haley collection)*

Over 100 years ago, in 1891 to be exact, a horsecar of the short-lived Main Avenue Railway treads its way up the street. The "Strictly First Class" Strater Hotel, built in 1888, continues in the 1990s to provide a haven of rest for tourists who come to ride the world-famous Durango & Silverton Narrow Gauge Railroad. *(Center of Southwest Studies, Fort Lewis College, Durango)*

(right) Car 7 and its crew rest at the end of the line in Animas City. *(W. Morris Cafky collection)*

A Durango Railway & Realty Company token is shown twice its actual size. *(Syd Joseph collection)*

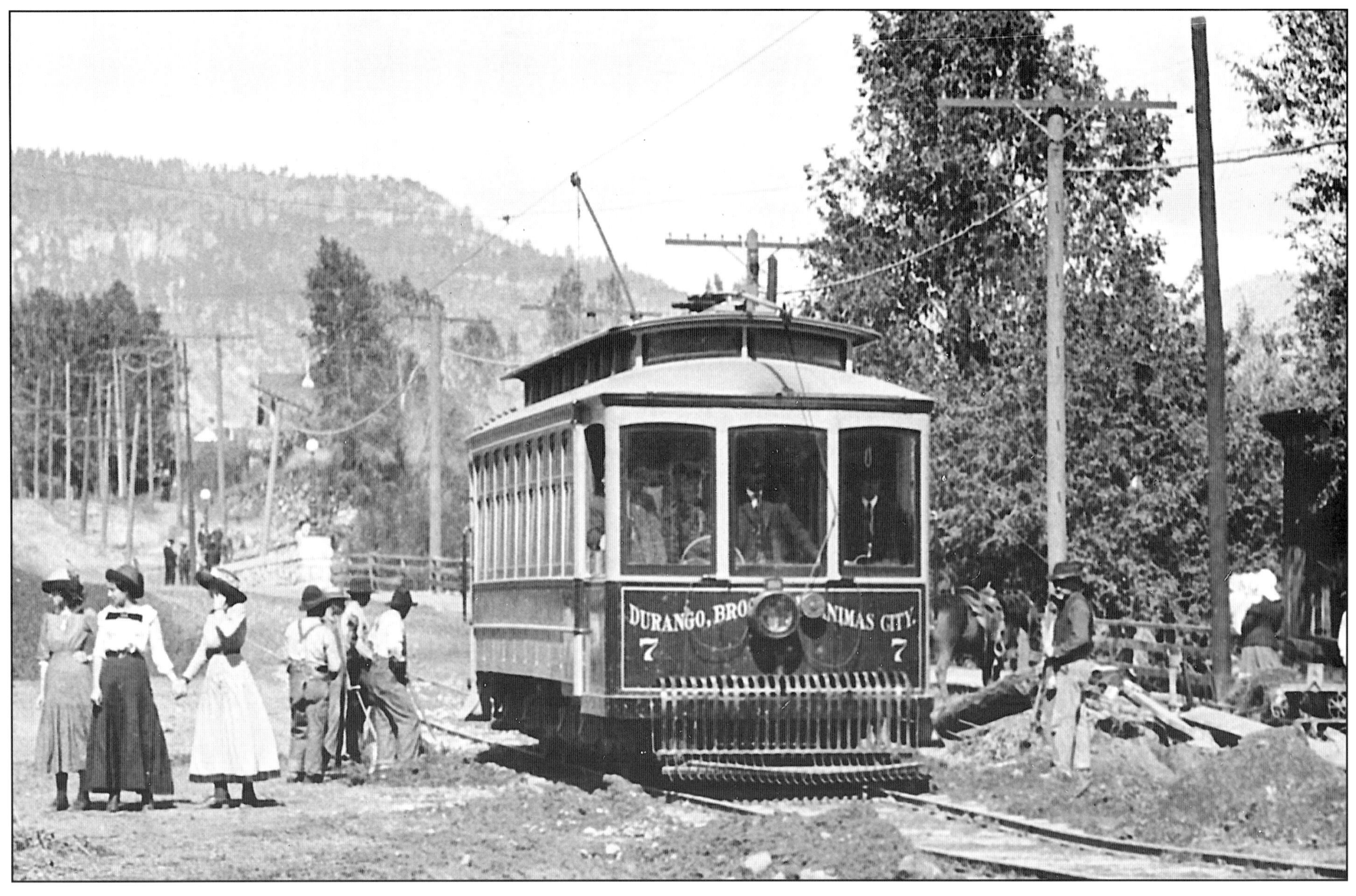

Debris from an October 1911 flood is being cleared away while work goes on to repair the damage to the track of the Durango Railway & Realty Company. The three ladies on the left seem to have their attention drawn to other matters as car 7 makes its way through the clutter. *(Animas Museum, La Plata County Historical Society)*

THE FIRST HORSE CAR IN DENVER, WHICH HAS CARRIED PEOPLE FOR OVER 40 YEARS AND IS STILL DOING BUSINESS. THE HORSE DRAWS THE CAR UP THE HILL AND RIDES DOWN.
#24. DENVER COLO. ELLISON PHOTO

CHERRELYN HORSECAR LINE

Sometime in 1893, a Denver City Railway horsecar was purchased for use on the Cherrelyn horsecar line which was built up the Broadway hill from Hampden to Quincy avenues in Englewood. As the years went by, the car's appearance deteriorated from bad to worse, but still the people rode it. During its later years the line became somewhat of a curiosity and was referred to as the "Gravity & Bronco" street railroad. Record books do not show the owner(s), but there is a ticket in existence that has the name of Harriette L. Bogue as manager printed on it. On January 7, 1900, it was reported that John Bogue (Harriette's husband?) was the driver and the horse's name was Quickstep.

It can only be speculated as to why the line was abandoned in November 1911, when it was such a curiosity, but it is safe to say that the equipment was totally worn out and there was not enough money in the farebox to continue operations. Another factor that may have proved fatal to the line was the opening of the Denver & South Platte Railway in 1908, which paralleled the entire route of the horsecar line. The amazing fact that it lasted as long as it did gives credit to the tenacious spirit of the owners.

But the story does not end there. The dilapidated horsecar body was purchased by G.G. Liebhart and moved to Rose Acres, his estate in suburban Edgewater, to become a playhouse for his children. The car remained at this location, its wheels and underframe buried in the ground, until 1950. Then Liebhart's daughter-in-law presented it to the local Rotary Club, which had it restored and put on display in Englewood's Civic Center. Although years of outdoor storage and neglect had taken its toll, the "cat" had not run out of lives. In 1988 the car was removed from display and completely refurbished, whereupon it was put on display inside the Cinderella City Shopping Center.

(previous page) Looking like a horse-drawn facsimile of Fontaine Fox's "Toonerville Trolley," the Cherrelyn horsecar prepares to leave the Englewood terminus. The photographer's caption is very exaggerated, as the Cherrelyn only ran from 1893 to 1911 and was not the first horsecar line in Denver.

(above) At the southern end of the line a ramp was used to allow the horse to back onto the car for the ride back down the hill.

(below) Horse and passengers enjoy the gravity ride. *(all, Colorado Historical Society)*

FORT COLLINS

FORT COLLINS

SOME OF MY BEST FRIENDS ARE STREETCARS

The above title is from an article that appeared in a 1947 issue of the *Saturday Evening Post* and leads off this brief story of the 44-year history of electric streetcars in Fort Collins.

A subsidiary of the Colorado & Southern Railway, the Denver & Interurban at one time had plans to develop an extended electric interurban line from the state capital to Fort Collins. Under-financed, the interurban was only able to reach Boulder and receive a franchise to build a city system in Fort Collins.

Two routes were under construction in 1907 but not completely ready for the electric cars. To provide service to the Race Meet and Stock Show, the line to the fairgrounds at Prospect Park was opened on August 28th, using a C&S steam switch engine pulling four open platform wooden coaches.

Fort Collins became a "streetcar town" on December 29, 1907, when four double-truck Woeber (Denver) built cars were put into service on College and Mountain avenues. In 1908 two additional streetcars and two trailers were ordered from the Jewett Car Company of Ohio, and a line was built to Lindenmeier Lake.

Continuing financial troubles beset the parent interurban company, and when it went into receivership it abruptly closed the Fort Collins system on July 10, 1918.

(previous page) College and Mountain avenues appeared thus in 1938. This intersection in the heart of downtown Fort Collins was the meeting place for the cars. *(Denver Public Library Western History Department)*

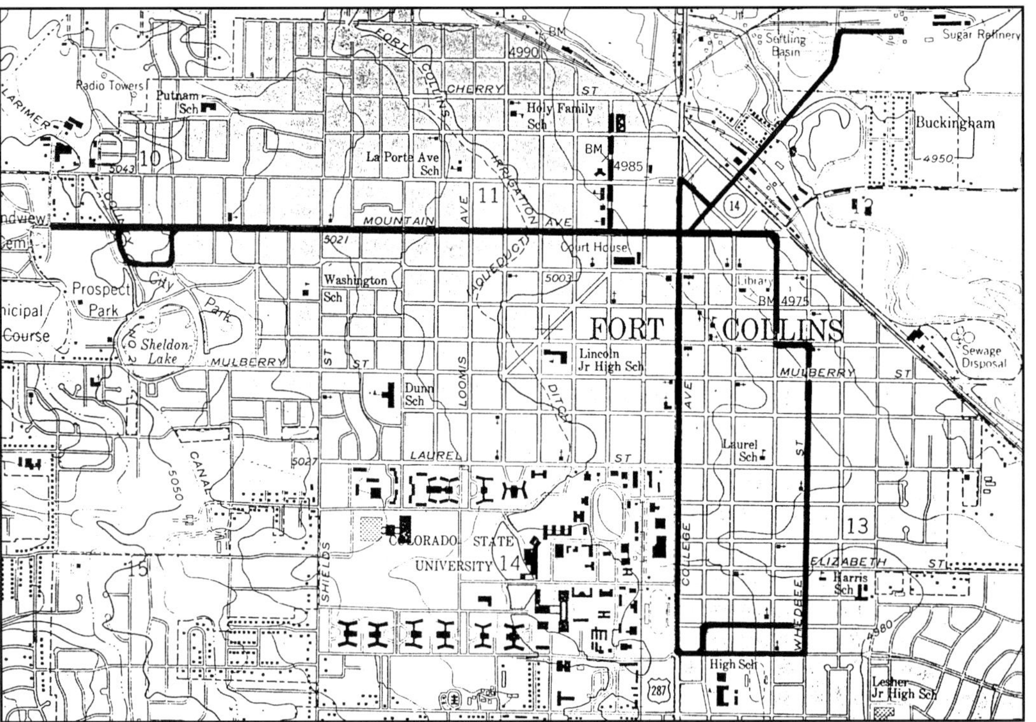

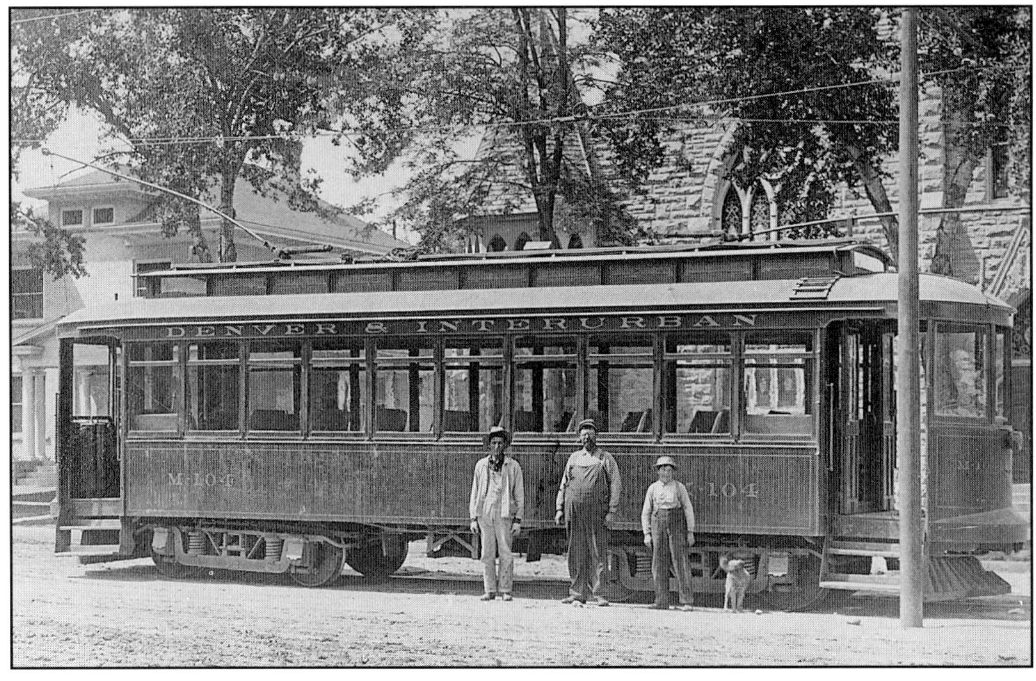

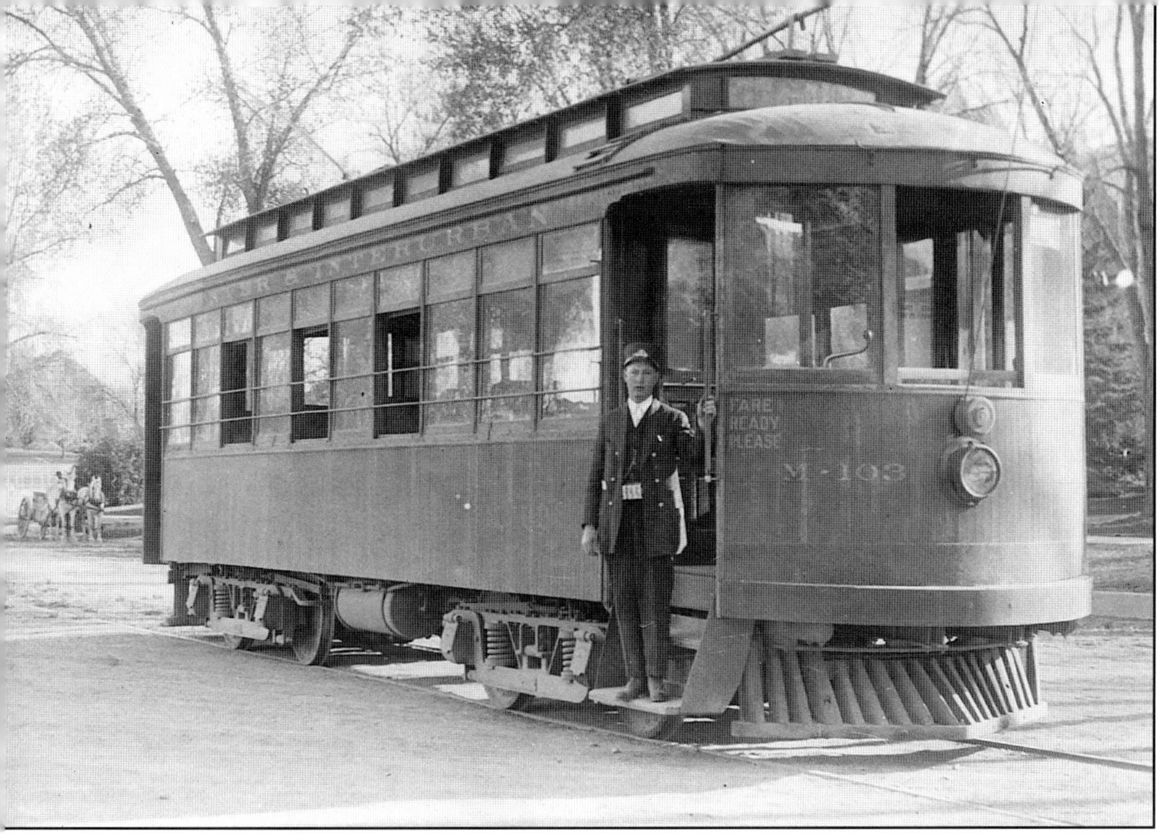

Car M-103, built by Woeber in Denver in 1907, is seen on College Avenue by the campus of what was then Colorado State Agricultural and Mining College. *(Fort Collins Public Library)*

Below is an enlargement of a Fort Collins Municipal Railway token. *(Syd Joseph collection)*

(opposite) In this 1909 view, car M-104 is eastbound on Mountain Avenue at Howes. A hostler and his helper are about to run the car the three blocks north on Howes to the carbarn. *(E.J. Haley collection)*

(right) Fort Collins was not spared the great blizzard of December 1913. A Jewett-built car is stalled in a mound of the white stuff. *(Fort Collins Public Library)*

Local newspapers were filled with editorials expounding on the value to the community of continued operation of the car lines. On January 7, 1919, an election was held proposing that the city buy and operate the system. The vote carried eight to one in favor of the purchase, and an accompanying bond issue for the necessary funds passed five to one. The majority of citizens had voted to keep their "friend."

Four new Birney one-man safety cars were purchased, the physical plant was renewed, schedules were adjusted and service resumed on May 24, 1919, Birney 21 made the first trial run.

The pro-trolley sentiment of the citizens remained strong throughout the existence of the system. On four occasions over the years, elections were held to determine the fate of the streetcars, and in every case the voters decided to keep the lines intact. In fact, the little cars were never voted off the streets, they just wore out. As the Birneys began to show their age and spare parts became impossible to obtain, by the late 1940s the system was reaching the end of its life span. It would have required a large infusion of money to completely rebuild the track and purchase new equipment. It just was not in the cards. The little system was put to rest on June 30, 1951—the last streetcar system to operate in the state of Colorado and the last in North America still using Birney cars.

(above right) Car 21 is eastbound on Pitkin Street at Mathews on June 23, 1951. *(E.J. Haley photo)*

Car 20 proceeds south along Mountain Avenue. *(Denver Public Library Western History Department)*

In one week the city-owned system will become history. Car 20 is on Howes Street, just down from the carbarn on June 23, 1951. This car was sold to the Pioneer Museum in Minden, Nebraska. *(E.J. Haley photo)*

In July 1939, Birney 26 heads south on College Avenue at Magnolia. This car was one of two purchased in 1922 from the defunct system in Cheyenne, Wyoming. It is now at Greenfield Village Museum in Dearborn, Michigan. *(Tom Gray photo, Don Robertson collection)*

The photographer has caught Birney 21 at a unique angle in downtown Fort Collins. As a source of additional revenue, theater ads prominently displayed on the cars' sides were a common fixture throughout most of the life of the trolleys. In this early 1950 view, Donald O'Connor and Jimmy Durante are starring in *The Milkman* at the Lyric Theater.

For such a small system the Fort Collins carbarn was quite impressive. Car 22 sits in front of the 1919 structure, waiting for its next run. In 1995, the barn is still standing, but in derelict condition. *(both, Museum collection)*

No, the sign on the front of the Birney has nothing to do with the frozen cubes one might use in a beverage. It was just a unique way to alert the population of Fort Collins that the lakes and ponds were not safe to use for skating. *(Museum collection)*

AN OLD FRIEND RETURNS

In 1984, thirty-three years after streetcars stopped running in Fort Collins and after a seven-year refurbishing project, Car 21 returned to life along a section of Mountain Avenue. The rebirth of the trolley is the work of members of the Fort Collins Municipal Railway Society. The public can ride the car on weekends and holidays from April to October. *(Al Kilminster photo, Fort Collins Municipal Railway Society collection)*

GRAND JUNCTION

GRAND JUNCTION

A GRAND BEGINNING

In 1881, a group of men from Gunnison headed by George A. Crawford—ex-governor of Kansas, frontier capitalist and land speculator with a reputation for establishing a new town "every decade or so"—staked out a townsite at the junction of the Gunnison and Grand (now Colorado) rivers. At first the settlement was called Ute, then West Denver and finally named Grand Junction for its site.

Incorporated in December 1881, within a month a store and saloon were built, and a ditch company was organized to supply water. Extension of the narrow gauge Denver & Rio Grande from Gunnison in 1882 gave the town its first rail outlet and assisted in stimulating growth. The first hotel, the Grand Junction House, was built in January 1882 and soon was joined by two rivals with the curious names of The Pig's Ear and The Pig's Eye. By year's end the town had almost 900 residents, several general stores, a drug store, two blacksmith shops, five hotels and restaurants, a meat market and 12 saloons. The predominance of "watering holes" was typical of all Western cattle towns, and Grand Junction was no less rowdy during its early years than similar settlements.

Grand Junction boomed when the standard gauge lines of the Colorado Midland and Denver & Rio Grande reached the community in 1890, establishing it as the prime trading center on the western slope of the Rocky Mountains.

(previous page) It appears to be market day in town as an interurban travels down Main Street. *(E.J. Haley collection)*

(above right) Charlie is providing the motive power for the advertising-bedecked horsecar. *(Horsecar, Grand Junction Street Railway Company, photographer unknown, circa 1890-1903, Mazzulla Collection, Amon Carter Museum, Fort Worth, Texas)*

A HORSE NAMED CHARLIE

Movement of the growing population within the city meant the need for transportation, and one of the town's most colorful characters of the period, Barney Kennedy, took on the challenge. He obtained a franchise, purchased and refurbished two used horsecars from Pueblo, laid rail along Main Street to the depot and opened for business on September 10, 1890.

For years afterward folks recalled one particular horse named Charlie, a large white steed that pulled the car until the line ceased operation on July 15, 1903. He became an object for photographers and newspaper items, and locals would vent their disapproval if they suspected that he was being ill-treated. When his service ended he was put out to a Mr. Bidwell's pasture to spend his remaining days in quiet and restful retirement.

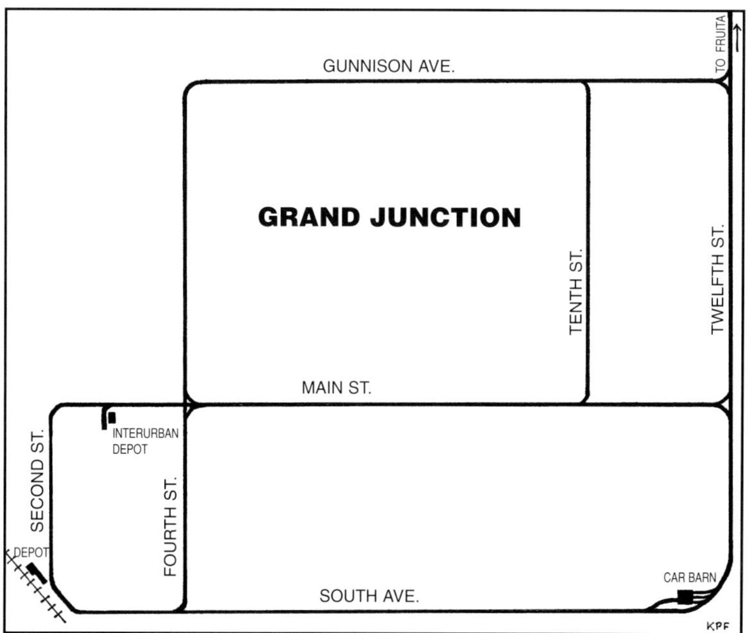

ELECTRIC CARS MAKE THEIR DEBUT

After the demise of the horsecar line, agitation set in to bring the town up to par with other cities, and that meant local transportation in the form of electric streetcars. But it would take almost six years before the advent of such service.

On May 22, 1909, at 5 a.m., early risers were treated to the spectacle of a test car making two passes over the line. Later that day the line was opened with the usual festivities. Townspeople could once again hold their heads high. Everything was Grand in the valley.

(above left) Here is another larger-than-life illustration of a token, this time a half fare of the Grand River Valley Railway. *(Syd Joseph collection)*

(left) The electric cars are draped in bunting for the first day of operation, May 22, 1909. *(E.J. Haley collection)*

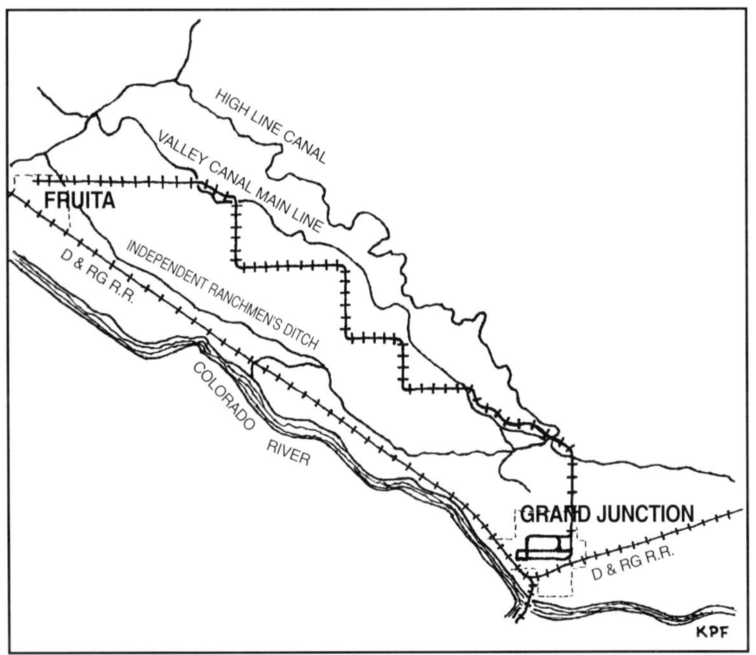

INTERURBAN COMES TO TOWN

In less then a year, July 14, 1910, an interurban line was completed to Fruita. It did not take a direct route but extended west in a zig-zag course (with nine sharp turns) along its 16-mile journey. Three interurban cars were built by the Woeber Carriage Company of Denver to accommodate passengers. The line also handled large shipments of fruit and vegetables from the fertile valley.

A NOT SO GRAND FINALE

By the mid-1920s, most of the riding public had deserted both the city line and interurban for the convenience of their automobiles. The former quit on October 29, 1926, and the latter on October 31, 1928, but electric freight service survived until January 1, 1935.

(above) Two new city cars were purchased from the Southern Car Company of High Point, North Carolina, in 1911. It looks as though a large contingency of the town's businessmen is inspecting the new car. *(GJ&GRV Ry. photo, E.J. Haley collection)*

(above left) The interior of interurban 76 was taken at the Woeber plant in Denver in May 1910, just before shipment to Grand Junction. *(Woeber Carriage Company photo, Kindig-Haley collection)*

(left) Interurban 51 was photographed in the late 1920s on Main Street between 3rd and 4th. *(Dean photo, E.J. Haley collection)*

(opposite page, top) Interurban 52 trailing a railroad coach, both jammed with first day riders on July 14, 1910, is at Fruita. *(Museum collection)*

(opposite, bottom) The map shows the zig-zag course of the line to Fruita.

The nickname of the interurban became the "Fruit Belt Route" as the line ran through orchards of apples, peaches and pears from the edge of Grand Junction to Fruita. Interurban 22 speeds along, circa 1910, passing workers picking the "fruits of their labor." *(E.J. Haley collection)*

CAMFIELD
CAMFIELD
HOTEL

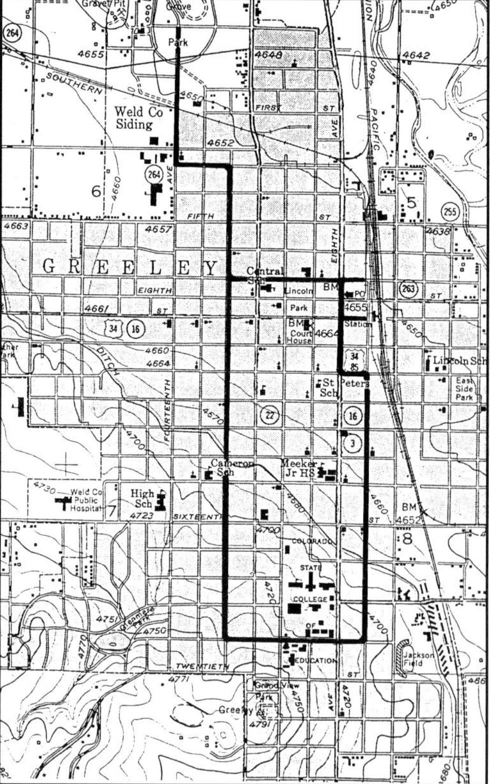

GREELEY

A UTOPIAN COMMUNITY

Conceived as a cooperative enterprise by and named for Horace Greeley, noted editor and publisher of the New York *Tribune*, the "Union Colony" was founded by his agricultural editor, Nathan C. Meeker. On March 15, 1870, the executive committee voted to name the town Greeley and chose a site at the junction of the Cache la Poudre and South Platte rivers.

Circulars were sent to prospective members, with Meeker stating that the idle, immoral, intemperate or inefficient need not apply. One of the "commandments" was: "Thou shalt not sell liquid damnation within the lines of Union Colony." This type of colony was based on the idea of a covenant community, a settlement based on voluntary association. People were to be united not by schemes of rapid riches but by utopian aspirations which were typically wedded to an agricultural community.

After several contested elections and court battles between 1872 and 1877, Greeley became the county seat and grew rapidly. The second electric light plant in the state was installed here in 1885, and at this time potato growing began on a large scale.

(previous page) Car 27 stands on Seventh Street, at the corner of Eighth Avenue, in front of the Camfield Hotel. The imposing structure began life as the Oasis Hotel in 1880, was purchased by D.A. Camfield for $25,000 in 1906, and its doors remained open for another 58 years. Both streetcar and hotel have ceased to exist; the trolley left the scene in 1922, the hotel site is now an unpaved parking lot. *(City of Greeley Museums: permanent collection)*

(above left) About the most pictorial activity one could achieve, on the diminutive system in Greeley, took place at the corner of Seventh Street and 12th Avenue. Car 26 is southbound on 12th while the unidentified car, turning from Seventh, heads northbound onto 12th for Island Grove Park. Notice the gentleman who is casually perched on the window sill at the back of the car. *(Ron Wittow collection)*

FROM A ONE HORSE TOWN TO A STREETCAR CITY

How one perceived a community, especially during its early growth period, was all important. Pride of place centered around the fact that a town could boast of having a modern hospital, a good school system, a large selection of retail establishments, an imposing city hall or court house and, right along with the times, a local transportation system. Greeley added the latter in 1910.

GREELEY & DENVER RAIL ROAD COMPANY

Construction began on the local car line in the spring of 1909, and the June 9th edition of the *Greeley Tribune* stated that, "Greeley woke up Tuesday morning and found a streetcar system unloaded at its very doors..." "The franchise which was given to this company calls for a line that will practically encircle the city and form a loop."

Because of several delays the system did not open for service until April 1910. Original equipment consisted of four secondhand cars from Spokane, Washington. The *Tribune* commented, "While not of the most modern type, the cars are comfortable coaches, and will afford a pleasing contrast to the cars in operation in some of Colorado's smaller cities."

For the first few years business was good. The company purchased two new single truck cars from the American Car Company of St. Louis in 1914.

FIRST

In Every

—Thing—

It costs nothing to ride on the street car---
if you come straight to the

and do your shopping. You can save more than car fare by trading with us

Good Goods--Small Profits--One Price to All

(above right) This advertisement appeared in the *Greeley Tribune*. *(E.J. Haley collection)*

Disaster struck the line on November 23, 1917 when flames consumed the carbarn, substation and three streetcars. From that point on, with limited finances and a deteriorating physical plant, the company limped along. Maintenance of the remaining cars, track and overhead wires was cut to a bare minimum. If it snowed, there more than likely would be no service. It finally came to a point that only car 30 was kept serviceable by using parts cannibalized from the other remaining car. On December 26, 1922, it broke down and never ran again.

Every kid loves a picnic, and what better way is there to get to the grove than on board a streetcar? It is July 22, 1921, and The Salvation Army has gathered a large contingency of the young population of the city. They are about to depart for Island Grove Park. The car they will be riding in is one of two (29 and 30) that the system purchased new in 1914 from American Car Company of St. Louis. *(City of Greeley Museums: permanent collection: Hazel E. Johnson)*

CLOTHING HOUSE
THE FAMOUS
CORNER BOOKSTORE
OPERA H
HERMITA
IMPORTED CIGARS
DETROIT PHOTOGRAPHIC CO.

LEADVILLE

HORSECAR RIDERS IN THE SKY

High up in the valley of the Arkansas, almost two miles above sea level, the camp that bore the nicknames of "Cloud City" and "Magic City" has had one of the richest histories, both monetarily and literarily, of any location in the Centennial State.

Known originally as Oro City but renamed Leadville, it was first a fabulous gold camp, then one of the richest silver camps, again a gold camp and lastly a producer of other mineral ores. The famous and infamous resided there: Horace Tabor, Baby Doe, Margaret (the unsinkable Molly) Brown, Jack Morrissey, Kitty Crawhurst, Madame Vestal, "Soapy" Smith and Mart Duggan, to name a few. And some of the mines became just as famous: Little Pittsburg, Matchless, Morningstar and Iron Silver.

During times of high activity in the mines the town's population would swell; when activity was on the downturn it was almost a ghost.

NOW YOU SEE IT ...

It was during the more prosperous times that a street railway was considered. Within a year of the city's incorporation at least seven organizations worked on plans to get their projects underway. But they all proved to be paper tigers. It was not until the summer of 1881, after two more false starts, that the City Railway Company (Leadville Street Railway Company, by some reports) was given a franchise and began construction in earnest. Track was put down along Harrison, from Chestnut to Eighth, then to Poplar and on to the Denver & Rio Grande depot. Four large horsecars capable of carrying 40 passengers, and painted white with blue roofs and green ends, were purchased. The grand opening, with leading citizens on hand, took place on August 5, 1881. During the summer the line did reasonably well, but the climate at Leadville's high altitude proved to be its nemesis.

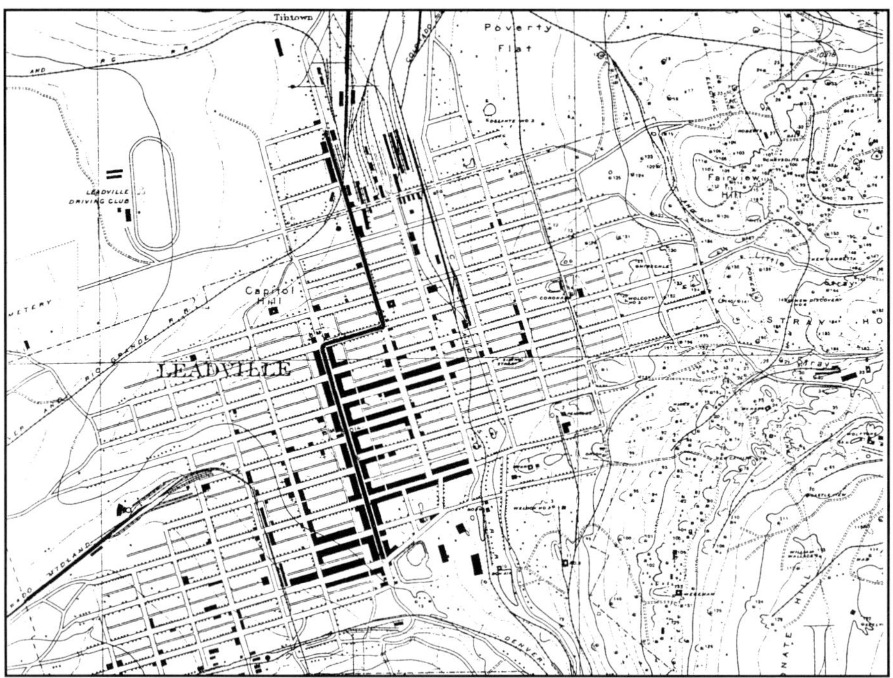

... NOW YOU DON'T

People joke that Leadville has "ten months of winter and two months mighty late in the fall." Leveler heads should have prevailed, with second thoughts given to the practicality of an animal-powered street railway in such an unfriendly environment. Not so, and it caused the company's undoing. As winter arrived and snow piled up, the company was unprepared to handle the situation. Three burros, used to pull each large car, were much too small (there was no money for replacement of either) and the *Leadville Herald* reported that, "... snow has formed a big obstacle, since it caked and froze on the tracks so rapidly that it was impossible for the employees to keep the road sufficiently clear." Runners replaced steel wheels under the cars, but they were still too heavy for the burros to handle. The unreliability of the service turned away any prospective riders, and by July 1882 the company was out of business.

(previous page) This photo is not meant to be a trick on the reader, even though it is very apparent there are no signs of track or horsecars in the scene looking south on Harrison Avenue. Research by untold numbers of historians has yet to unearth a view of the transitory horsecar operation of the City Railway Company in Leadville. *(Colorado Historical Society)*

LITTLETON

LITTLETON

Opened in 1908, the Denver & South Platte Railway was a five-mile streetcar system whose first section extended south, four and one-half miles, from a connection with the Denver Tramway on Broadway at Hampden in Englewood, to Rapp and Main streets in Littleton. The line operated in the center of Broadway and from Hampden to Quincy, paralleled the Cherrelyn horsecar line. In 1909, additional trackage was installed in Littleton and the line extended across the Platte River to Bowles Park. Built to the same gauge as the Tramway, for most of its life it leased equipment from the larger company. The Bowles Park extension remained in service until 1917, when the track was torn up and sold for scrap.

(previous page) Almost everyone's attention is focused on leased Denver Tramway car 232 as it turns off Prince Street to enter Littleton's Main Street, sometime around 1908. Jull's Hardware Store appears in the background. Above, car 243 is coming down Prince on its way into downtown Littleton.

At right, leased Denver Tramway car 243 crosses the Platte River after visiting Bowles Park. The white railings belong to the road bridge that carries Bowles Avenue over the river. *(all, Littleton Historical Museum)*

In 1919 the company purchased its own equipment, two single truck, Birney safety cars. By the mid-1920s increased use of automobiles caused a sharp loss of ridership, and after a stormy meeting held by the State Public Utilities Commission the line was authorized to abandon on May 5, 1926. The following year the diminutive cars were sold to York Utilities in Maine for use on that system. The cars escaped the scrap heap when the utility ceased operating and found their way to the Seashore Trolley Museum at Kennebunkport, Maine. Today, one car provides faithful service while its companion serves as a billboard pointing the way from U.S. 1 to the museum.

(above) Open car 127 proceeds westbound on Main, with a banner on its tender advertising "Jefferies & Johnson's last week at the Tabor Grand" in Denver. *(Littleton Historical Museum)*

(left) Car 232 coasts down Slaughterhouse Gulch. The scene is a fairly early one in the life of the system, since the track has yet to be ballasted. *(E.J. Haley collection)*

Denver & South Platte Railway's Birney car 1 was purchased from American Car Company of St. Louis in 1919. It stands on Littleton's Main Street, just east of Rapp, waiting for its departure time on the run to Englewood. The tile-roofed building in the background served as the town's library until 1965. As of 1995 it remains standing but vacant. *(E.J. Haley collection)*

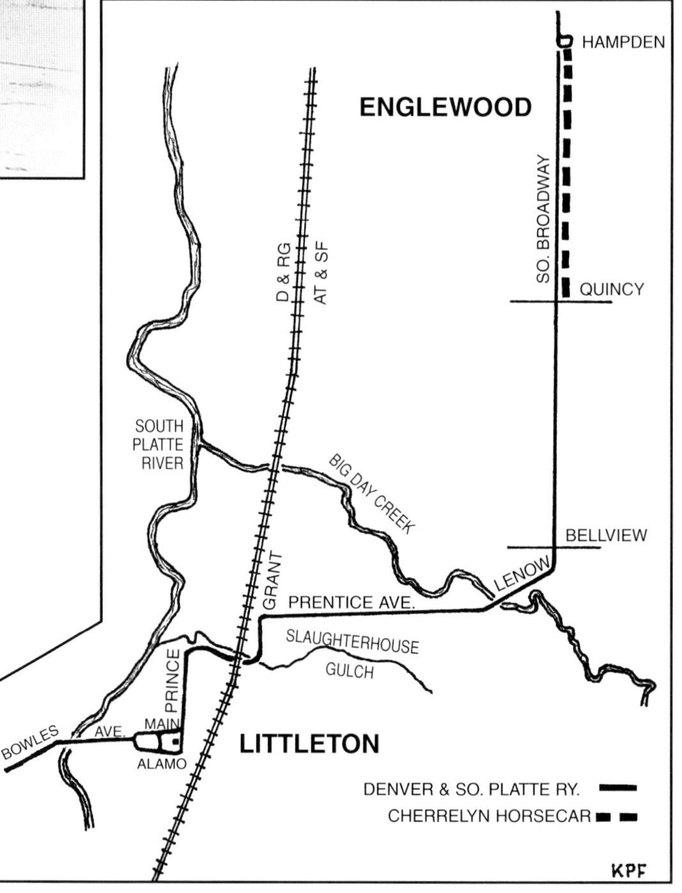

MANITOU SPRINGS

MANITOU SPRINGS

AT THE FOOT OF PIKES PEAK

Although the presence of soda springs was known by French traders as early as the 1830s it was not until 1872, with the building of a resort hotel by Dr. William A. Bell and General William Jackson Palmer, that the area now known as Manitou Springs became popular.

THE "DINKY"

During 1891, the Manitou & Pikes Peak Railway (the cog railway) was completed from Ruxton Avenue to the summit of Pikes Peak. Unfortunately, the railway's base station was some distance from the center of the community and required prospective tourists to negotiate a long uphill hike from the Denver & Rio Grande depot.

Senator M.A. Leddy thought that the establishment of a trolley line between the railroad station and cog depot would have a guaranteed ridership. In the summer of 1893 he asked for and received a franchise allowing the Manitou Electric Railway & Casino Company to construct a single track, electric trolley line between the two points. The line as originally built was slightly over a mile and a half in length and used two single-truck open and one closed car to transport tourists from the Rio Grande depot and a connection with the Colorado Springs streetcar company to the cog railway.

Late in 1895 the line was leased to the Colorado Springs Rapid Transit Company. In 1901, when W.S. Stratton acquired the CSRT, he inherited this short line, cut its trackage back to Manitou and Ruxton avenues and extended his Colorado Springs & Interurban to that intersection. After Stratton's death in 1902 the little line became independent. The "Dinky" as some folks called it, never earned much of a profit and on Labor Day in 1928 made its final run.

(previous page) Car 2 stands beside the stone waiting station opposite the Cog Road depot. The trolleys shuttled back and forth between Manitou Springs and the cog railway as fast as possible during the tourist season. *(Donald Duke collection)*

(above) Car 1 is at the terminal at Ruxton and Manitou avenues in Manitou Springs. *(E.J. Haley collection)*

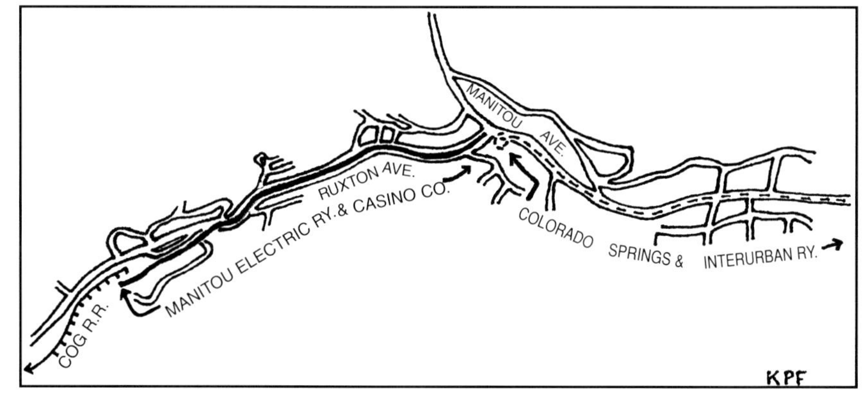

Open car 9 passes the Ute Iron Spring pavilion on its way to a connection with the Colorado Springs line in Manitou Springs. The photo was taken around 1895 when the trolley terminated alongside the tracks of the cog railway depot. A few years later the bridge across Ruxton Creek was abandoned, and the trolley rerouted along the south bank of the creek to a new stone station. *(Horace Poly photo, Denver Public Library Western History Department)*

(right) A westbound open car pauses at Soda Spring on its way to the cog depot. The Cliff House resort hotel appears in the background. The photograph was taken prior to 1901 when the "Dinky" still operated to the Denver & Rio Grande depot in Manitou Springs. *(E.J. Haley collection)*

Here is the Manitou and Ruxton intersection again, around 1906. Colorado Springs & Interurban car 60 has its trolley pole reversed and is ready to return to Colorado Springs. The dinky has just arrived from the cog depot with passengers making a connection to the big car. *(Mrs. Jean Campbell collection)*

MARBLE

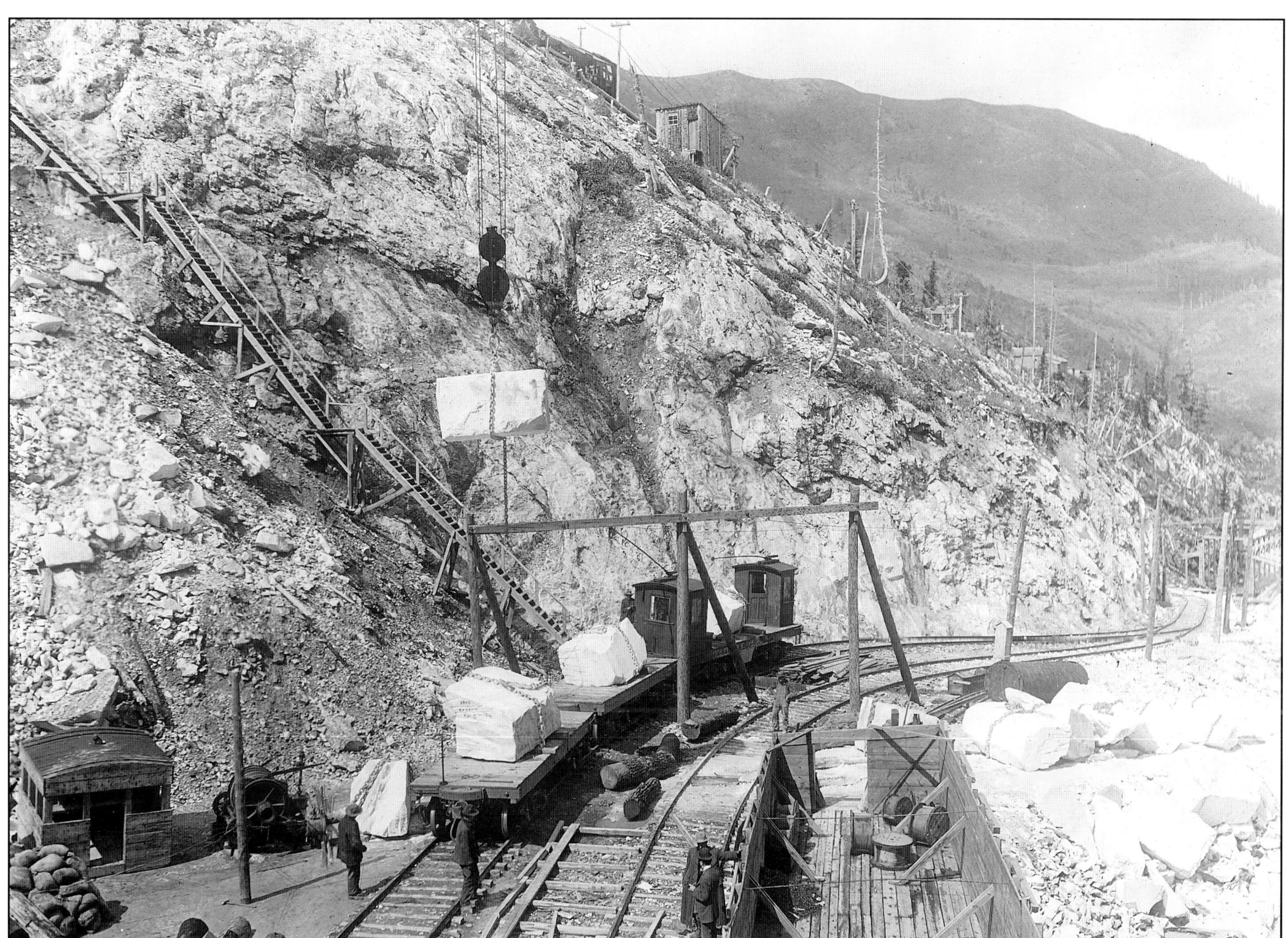

MARBLE

HARD ROCK

A production that took over 60 million years to complete, and produced some of the hardest rock known to man, was not discovered until 1882. Lured into the isolated upper reaches of the Crystal River Valley by the prospect of finding gold and silver, instead prospectors discovered monumental deposits of pure white marble. But it was not until 1905 that serious attempts were made to find a way to extract the highly prized building material.

Colonel Channing F. Meek was the one who succeeded in overcoming the hazardous venture of bringing the marble out of the high mountains; before he was through he would spend over three million dollars developing the quarries, mill and transportation.

Securing a path from the outside world into the secluded valley was another obstacle to overcome. Colonel Meek signed a lease for a previously surveyed right-of-way between Placita and Marble and built the Crystal River & San Juan Railroad. The Colorado-Yule Marble Company was established in 1906, a mill was constructed in the valley, and by 1907 the first blocks of marble were being wagoned down from the quarry. Wagons and horses were replaced by a Chase Steam Tractor in 1908, and then in the fall the company widened the roadway for construction of an electric tramway.

STEEP GRADES UNDER A THIN WIRE

In 1910 a 3.9-mile, standard gauge electric line was opened, and two work cars began bringing monumental chunks of white rock down grades as steep as 17 percent. These grades, considered extremely steep for any type of railroad, were responsible for several spectacular and sometimes fatal accidents during the line's history. One accident, which took place on August 12, 1912, claimed the life of Colonel Meek.

DIMINISHING RETURNS

Although the quarry was noted for yielding high quality marble that was used in building many historical monuments and structures, new building materials began replacing the need for quality marble in the 1920s. After purchase by Vermont Marble Company in 1928, a diminishing market and high production costs ultimately led to the closure of the operation in September 1941.

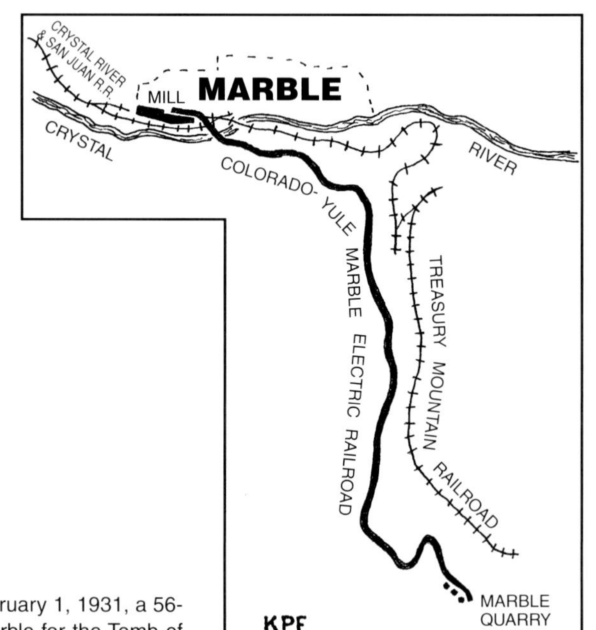

(below) On February 1, 1931, a 56-ton block of marble for the Tomb of the Unknown Soldier was moved down the mountain. It was skidded on two small wheels and an oak timber, moving one mile per day. *(E.J. Haley collection)*

(previous page) A hoist is loading marble onto a flat car for the trip to the mill. Several blocks can be seen stored on the ground to the right. Workers were cutting marble out of the quarry faster than the electric tram could haul it out. *(George L. Beam photo, E.J. Haley collection)*

PUEBLO

WOMEN'S READY-TO-WEAR
THE UNIQUE
524 No. MAIN-THE UNIQUE-524 No. MAIN
THE UNIQUE
UNION
FAIRMOUNT PARK
SMOKE HOUSE
BILLIARDS
THE RAY-MOCH CLOTHING CO.

PUEBLO

The first recorded explorers came to the area which is now the city of Pueblo in 1706. Although many years would pass before a permanent settlement was established, the future site of Pueblo was frequented by traders, trappers, shepherds, priests, soldiers and prospectors.

Lieutenant Zebulon Pike camped in the area in 1806. Trapper and trader Major Jacob Fowler built a three-room log house in 1822 but moved on. Finally, in 1842 James P. Beckworth built a trading post and is credited with the settlement and naming of the community.

A group of prospectors arrived in 1858 from St. Louis and established the town of Fountain City, now part of Pueblo. The rival town of Pueblo City was laid out by Denver promoters in 1860. By 1870 it was incorporated as a town with a population of 700. The narrow gauge Denver & Rio Grande was extended into the area in 1872, and one year later the town of South Pueblo was incorporated. In 1876 the Santa Fe railroad reached the area and in 1887 was extended to Denver. The growth of the area became extraordinary.

STEEL TOWN TROLLEYS

The Pueblo Street Railway was organized in 1879, and by 1880 horse drawn cars were running several blocks up Santa Fe from Second. Colorado Coal & Iron (now CF&I Steel) opened its first blast furnace in 1881, a third Pueblo community—Central Pueblo—was incorporated in 1882, and the Mather and Geist smelter was built. The Eilers smelter opened the next year, all three communities were consolidated as one in 1886, and the Guggenheim smelter was opened in 1888. Pueblo was rightly called "Steel City of the West."

Electric streetcar service began on June 6, 1890, and at the height of rail service the company operated over 35 miles of track. Lines served the steel mills, Lake Minnequa, Fairmount and City parks.

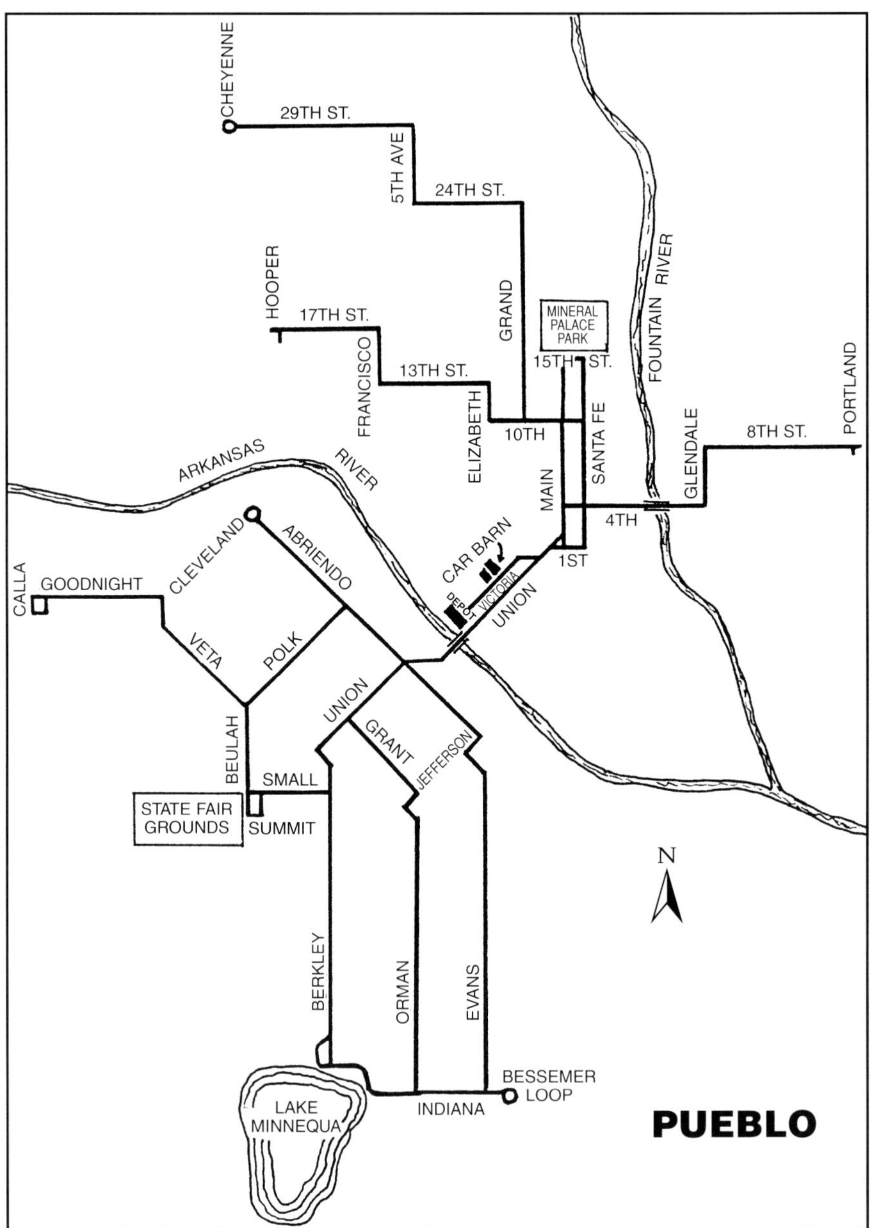

(previous page) Car 74, built by American Car Company of St. Louis in 1912, stops on Main Street at Sixth to let off a passenger. The Thatcher Building is the six-story structure on the right, and the tower of the Grand Opera House can be seen in the distance. The Grand was completely destroyed by fire on March 1, 1922. *(Colorado Historical Society)*

A STREETCAR NAMED BIRNEY

Serious ridership losses began in the early 1920s due to the prosperity of the steel business and the consequent widespread use of private automobiles. To combat the rising costs of operation, coupled with a 24 percent drop in ridership over a period of five years, the company began replacing its fleet of double truck cars with single truck Birney Safety Cars. Eleven were received new during 1920–1923, and in 1935 the company bought 24 used Birneys from the defunct system in Colorado Springs. When these cars were placed in service, the double truckers were retired.

Had not the company taken drastic measures to enable it to continue serving the public, it is doubtful that the lines would have survived the Great Depression. The World War II era brought an upsurge in ridership and a challenge to keep equipment, that was beginning to show its age, on the street. After the hostilities were over and prosperity returned, ridership began its slide once again. With no prospects of being able to compete with the glut of new auto ownership, the company applied for abandonment of the remaining car lines.

The grand finale would come during the month of November 1947. On Saturday, November 8th, a "Wheels of Progress" pageant and parade wound its way through downtown to celebrate the change over from streetcar to bus. The *Pueblo Star-Journal* reported that thousands witnessed the event, and that a luncheon was held at the Vail Hotel attended by Hollywood actress Jorja Curtwright, city and county officials, representatives of General Motors and officials of the power company and Chamber of Commerce. In the waning hours of that day the Lake Minnequa/24th-Grand/Fairmount Park line, along with the Orman Avenue/Irving Place line, were abandoned.

But not until November 29 would the last Birneys be put to rest. The final hurrah was consigned to Pueblo's busiest car line which served the Park Hill neighborhood, Mesa Junction and down Evans Avenue to Bessemer Loop.

The street has yet to be paved as an early single-truck streetcar makes its way up Santa Fe Avenue. *(E.J. Haley collection)*

A double enlargement of Pueblo Electric Street Railway's half-fare token good for children under 12 years. *(Syd Joseph collection)*

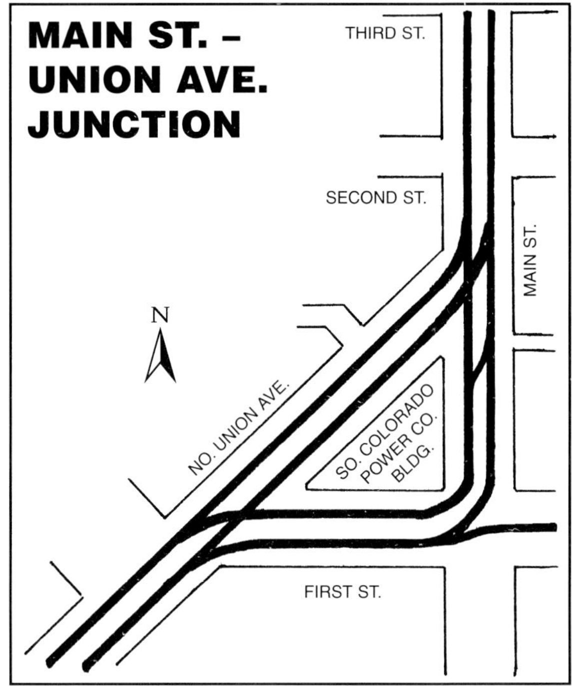

MAIN-UNION JUNCTION

(above) From the early days of electric streetcar operation the Main-Union junction was always a busy and interesting place. Looking north from First Street, up Main, the crowded open car is clustered with advertising signs. The roof advertises the Pueblo Carriage Company while the dash denotes a coming balloon ascension. The structure on the left, with bays and cupola, eventually contained offices for the transit company.

(right) Looking northeast, up Union toward Main, a man on a white steed appears to be racing the Lake Minnequa car to the Santa Fe Railway crossing. *(both Furman photos, Pueblo Library District)*

It is difficult to tell whether the object of the photographer's picture was the Erickson Building or Pueblo & Suburban Traction & Light Company's streetcar 27. Nevertheless, he was able to attract just about everyone's attention as the camera records the scene for posterity at the corner of Evans and Northern avenues. *(Denver Public Library Western History Department)*

Looking north on Main Street at First. Only one horse-drawn delivery wagon appears, left of the streetcar, as automobiles outnumber all else. The five-story building on the right is the historic Central Block. It contained an interior open rotunda extending the full height of the structure. The building was consumed by fire one night in August 1953. *(Colorado Historical Society)*

The June 1921 floods on the Arkansas River and Fountain Creek devastated many parts of Pueblo. The force of the water is graphically portrayed in this scene on Main Street near Third. Debris and parts of buildings clutter the street along with five damaged streetcars. The streetcars were eventually repaired and a few survived until the mid-1930s. *(E.J. Haley collection)*

Transition on Main Street. Many citizens have altered their method of transport to the automobile, and the contraptions are beginning to obstruct the movement of the trolleys. In an attempt to counter the loss in ridership Birney Safety Cars were introduced. In this circa 1925 view one of the 84-90 series is northbound on its way to Irving Place as double-truck car 61 approaches the camera bound for Bessemer Loop. *(Colorado Historical Society)*

The salesman from Cincinnati Car Company must have been more convincing as almost all Birneys that were purchased in Colorado came from that company. The first to arrive in Pueblo, in 1921, were Nos. 80-83 which were originally used on the stub-end lines from Union and Abriendo. As the fleet increased and replaced the double-truck cars, they were assigned to all lines. Pueblo's first Birney, No. 80, rests at the Irving Place wye on 17th Street at Hooper. The motorman has changed the route number and destination for the car's southbound trip to Bessemer Loop via Orman Avenue. *(Museum collection) (inset)* It is obvious that the Cincinnati Car Company did not expend a great deal of money on advertising as is shown by this ad which appeared in the October 21, 1916, issue of the *Electric Railway Journal. (both, Museum collection)*

Of the entire group of Birneys that operated in Pueblo (at least 34) only Nos. 84-90 were built by American Car Company, a subsidiary of the J.G. Brill Company. This small group could be quickly identified from the rest of Pueblo's Birneys by the globe ventilators on the roof and the two marker lights on the front letterboard. Car 86 picks up a few passengers in front of the Colorado Theater on Main Street. *(inset)* This is one of the earliest known advertisements of the original Birney, that was promoted by the J.G. Brill Company, in the July 15, 1916, issue of the *Electric Railway Journal. (both, Museum collection)*

East Eighth Street, in the Park Hill neighborhood, is undergoing repairs as car 120 gingerly makes its way past the construction site at La Crosse. The patriotic dash sign dates this picture to the World War II era. *(W.C. Whittaker photo, Don Robertson collection)*

Transit systems throughout the country painted equipment in patriotic advertising during World War II. Car 132 was also offering a "free ride" with the purchase of a 25-cent War Stamp. *(W.C. Whittaker photo, Don Robertson collection)*

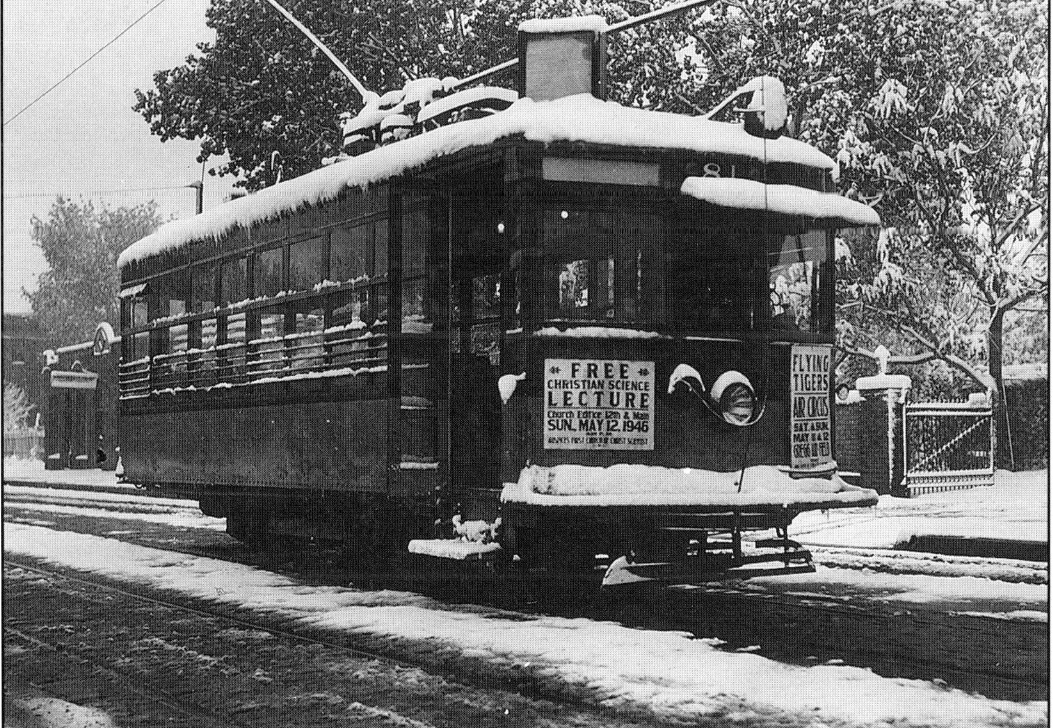

It can snow just about any month in Colorado. To prove the point, an early May 1946 storm has deposited the sticky white stuff all over car 81. An optimistic advertisement on the right programs, "Flying Tigers Air Circus," coming to Gregg Air Field, May 11th and 12th. *(Museum collection)*

Not all things seem as they appear. As a case in point, if you look closely at this photo what looks like a streetcar is in reality an ersatz facsimile of a Birney on rubber tires! It was built by the street railway employees for the 1928 Labor Day parade. The "vehicle," along with the mule which has a sign proclaiming "Streetcar Motor, 1890," is alongside the track on Victoria at C Street. *(City of Pueblo, Department of Transportation)*

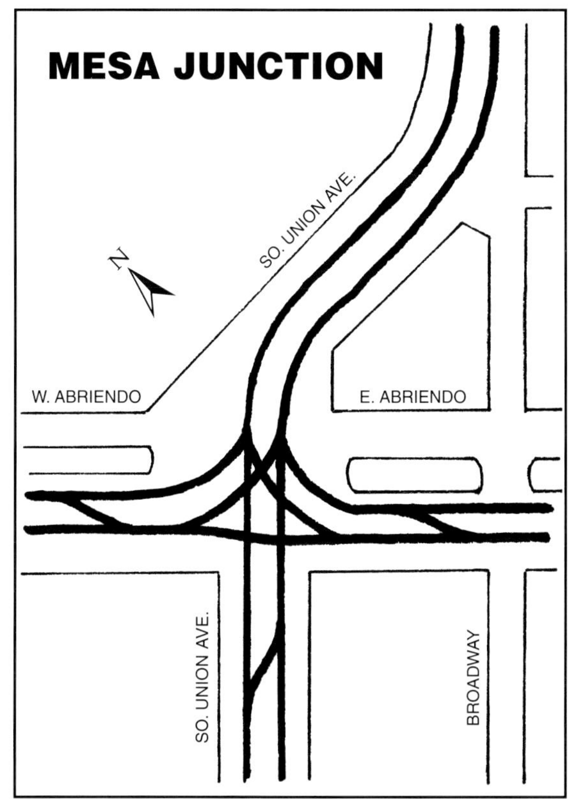

MESA JUNCTION

From 1914 until just before the attack on Pearl Harbor in 1941, when the three stub-end lines (all numbered 15) were abandoned, Mesa Junction was an important transfer point for all three through routes and the ubiquitous Routes 15.

(above) Car 120, on the short turn Route 4 (24th & Grand) crosses Abriendo on Union on its way to downtown. Car 113, signed for Route 2 will follow. *(Museum collection)*

(left) Car 81 has stub-ended at Union, the motorman has changed the pole and is ready to travel northwest on Abriendo on one of the Routes 15. *(Pueblo District Library)*

Car 116 zips up the South Union Avenue hill, on its way toward Mesa Junction and its final destination at Bessemer Loop, as car 124 prepares to cross the Union Avenue Bridge on its way downtown. Although all Birneys that came to Pueblo were of the double-end variety, most were equipped to run as single-end with route box numbers, roof bells and visors only on one end. *(John W. Maxwell photo)*

Two Pueblo Birneys remain a puzzle. Nos. 91 and 92 do not fit into the sequence of cars that were obtained second-hand from Colorado Springs (112-134) nor were they among the cars (80-90) purchased new for the system. Could it be that they were renumbered from a pair of cars that was involved in a particularly bad mishap? The question mark remains. Here mystery car 91 has left Mesa Junction behind and ambles down the South Union Avenue hill on its way downtown as car 80 exits the photo on the left. *(John W. Maxwell photo)*

Car 121 has a full load of passengers as it trundles down Grand near 15th Street. The structure on the left is the coach house (now a restaurant) of the J.A. Thatcher mansion (now a museum) *(Museum collection)*

Car 88 passes over a stretch of single track in an unpaved street next to a spiffy looking Plymouth coupe. In 1995, the body of this particular Birney and its cousin, car 84, were located on a ranch, have been moved to town and are scheduled for restoration. *(Museum collection)*

Car 131 has just completed the loop at Minnequa Park. At one time the company owned a station, of frame and brick construction, that was located at the loop. The motorman has changed the route number and destination for the trip north to Fairmount Park on 29th Street. *(Museum collection)*

Two car lines served the Colorado Fuel & Iron Company steel plant at Bessemer Loop. One ran down Orman Avenue, then east on Indiana to the loop, while the other line came down Evans. The plant's employees generated a lot of business for the trolleys until a few years after World War II when automobiles once again became readily available. The ad on the car is for an air show at Gregg Airfield and BATMAN is one of the stunt flyers. *(Museum collection)*

The weekly baseball schedule is prominently displayed on car 116 as it makes its way through the heart of the retail and commercial section on Main Street. In 1995 the trolleys have long since departed the scene, the street has been repaved and made into a one-way, most of the businesses have closed, and the Colorado Theater no longer shows movies. Capitulation to the automobile and its insatiable appetite for space, and the dispersal of commercial enterprises to accommodate it, proved the undoing and ultimate decline of the more centrally located downtown. *(Museum collection)*

Birney 118 is eastbound on its way to the Park Hill neighborhood while crossing the East Fourth Street Bridge over the Denver & Rio Grande Western Railroad and Fountain Creek. *(Gene McKeever collection)*

Birney car 125 has just picked up a passenger on Fifth Avenue at 27th Street in North Pueblo. Most of the Birneys, as well as the track gauge of Pueblo, were somewhat unusual. About 20 cars were converted to single-end operation, and all 35 had large route number boxes and gongs mounted on the roof. They also had a ladder on one side which gave access to the roof, a visor placed over the middle and left front windows, and a grab rail affixed to the anticlimber on the front. The track gauge of four feet was used by very few systems; San Antonio and Honolulu were two of them. *(E.J. Haley collection)*

TRINIDAD

TRINIDAD

A TOUGH PLACE

Almost all frontier towns had a reputation for being places of action. Whether it was from the roll of a little steel ball on a roulette table or the race of fortune hunters to stake claims on plots of earth that chance could make millionaires or a shoot-out over a card game, the settlement of the west was "wild and woolly."

Named for the daughter of a pioneer settler, Trinidad was chosen Las Animas county seat in 1866, at a time when it was overflowing with settlers, traders and desperadoes of all descriptions. The so called "Battle of Trinidad" took place on Christmas Day in 1867, when a wrestling match developed into a riot that involved almost a thousand people. It took weeks, martial law and cavalry from Fort Lyon and Fort Reynolds to calm things down. Trinidad became known as a "tough place."

BLACK DIAMONDS, CATTLE AND MULECARS: OH MY

It was not gold or silver that put the town on the map but the discovery of "black diamonds" which attracted folks and swelled the population. Frank Bloom opened the first coal mine in the district in 1867, and additional mines started up as demand increased with the building of smelters throughout the state and the steel mills at Pueblo. With the arrival of the railroads and attendant shipping facilities, the cattle industry was stimulated and flourished for the next two decades. The Trinidad Street Railway was formed and by 1888 had a mile and a half of track, two cars and eight mules. In 1891 an additional mile and a half of track was in use, six cars were on the roster and the motive power was replaced by 35 horses.

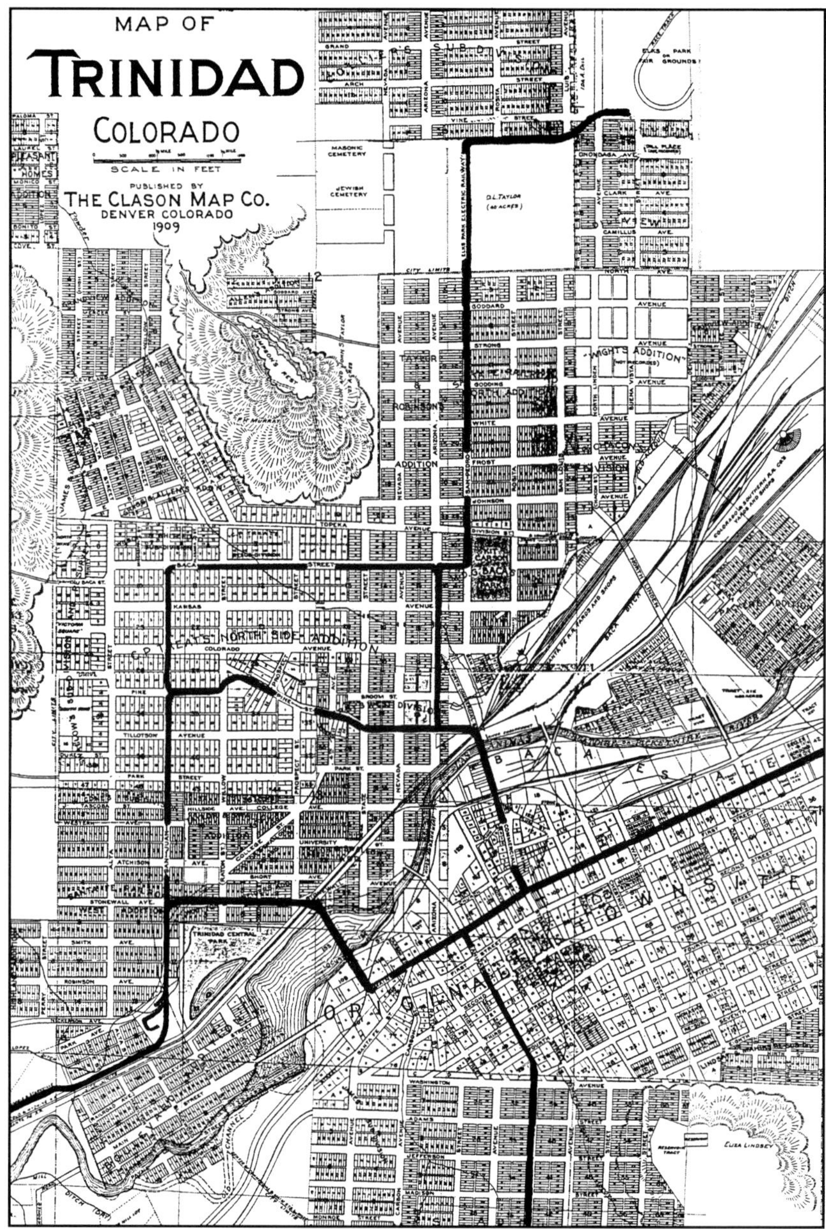

(previous page) The complete roster of the Trinidad Electric Transmission Railway & Gas Company's three interurban cars (1,2 and 6) meets at the junction of the Starkville and Cokedale lines. *(Colorado Historical Society)*

Looking south, Trinidad Street Railway's two bob-tail horsecars stand on the iron truss bridge that carried Commercial Street over the Purgatory River. The sign above the right hand bridge portal states, "$10 Fine For Driving Faster Than A Walk Over This Bridge. Keep To The Right." A Trinidad landmark, Fisher's Peak, is visible through the cross bracing at the far end of the bridge. *(Aultman Studio photo, E.J. Haley collection)*

Gas lamps are being installed on East Main Street as horsecar 2 crests the hill. Conflicting industry publications of the era list the company as using the unusual track gauge of three feet, two inches or three feet. All reports agree on the weight of the rail as being 14 pounds per yard. Needless to say, construction was of a very flimsy nature, whatever the gauge, and the rail in this photo looks as if it were glued in place using a bargain brand. *(Aultman Studio photo, Colorado Historical Society)*

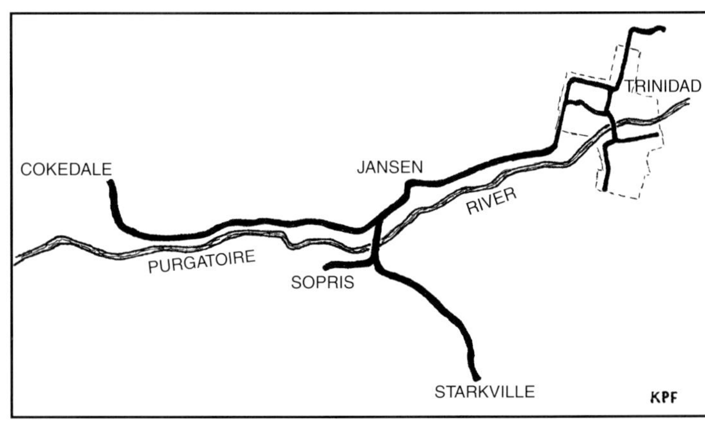

TOWN AND COUNTRY TRAMS

In 1904 the horsecar system was abandoned and an electric railway constructed. The Trinidad Electric Railway & Gas Company built five miles of city, and nine miles of interurban track and opened on April 28th. City cars served the county fairgrounds, East Main, a loop line (via Baca, San Juan, Pine and Arizona) and Central Park. The interurban passed through mountainous country requiring a number of curves and grades to reach Sopris and Starkville. Five city and three interurban cars were put into service on opening day when between 6,000 and 7,000 people were carried during the celebration. In 1908 the interurban was extended to Cokedale, and additional trackage was added to the city lines. The company became the property of Federal Light & Traction in 1911, and the local name was changed to Trinidad Electric Transmission Railway & Gas Company.

By 1920 use of the automobile had so reduced ridership on the city cars that the company began filing requests with the Colorado Public Utilities Commission to abandon them. Authorization was finally received in January 1922 and accordingly on March 12, the interurban was rerouted and the local lines closed. The interurban would struggle on until it too was abandoned on September 15, 1923.

(above) Sometime prior to 1905 a streetcar trundles down unpaved Commercial Street, past the Trinidad Hotel, climbing the grade to the bridge across the Purgatory River on the Baca Loop line. *(Colorado Historical Society)*

(above left) A double enlargement of Trinidad Street Railway's five-cent token. *(Syd Joseph collection)*

(middle left) Car 9, built by Woeber in 1912, waits for a train crossing Commercial. *(Colorado Historical Society)*

(bottom left) Electric locomotive 24 was built in 1907. One of its duties was to bring loaded coal cars from the Santa Fe Railway to the company power plant, a job which continued until mid-1949 over a limited amount of trackage. *(Colorado Historical Society)*

(opposite page, top left) The corner of Commercial and Main was a transfer point between car lines. The pole in front of Hausman's Drug Store has a board containing schedules. *(Colorado Historical Society)*

(top right) The map shows approximate location of the interurban line to Cokedale, Sopris and Starkville.

(bottom right) On the morning of October 24, 1906, frost on the rail along the eight percent grade on the Animas Street hill caused car 7 to go out of control and plow into the corner of the West Block Building. Luckily no one was seriously injured but the streetcar was a total loss. *(Aultman Studio photo, E.J. Haley collection)*

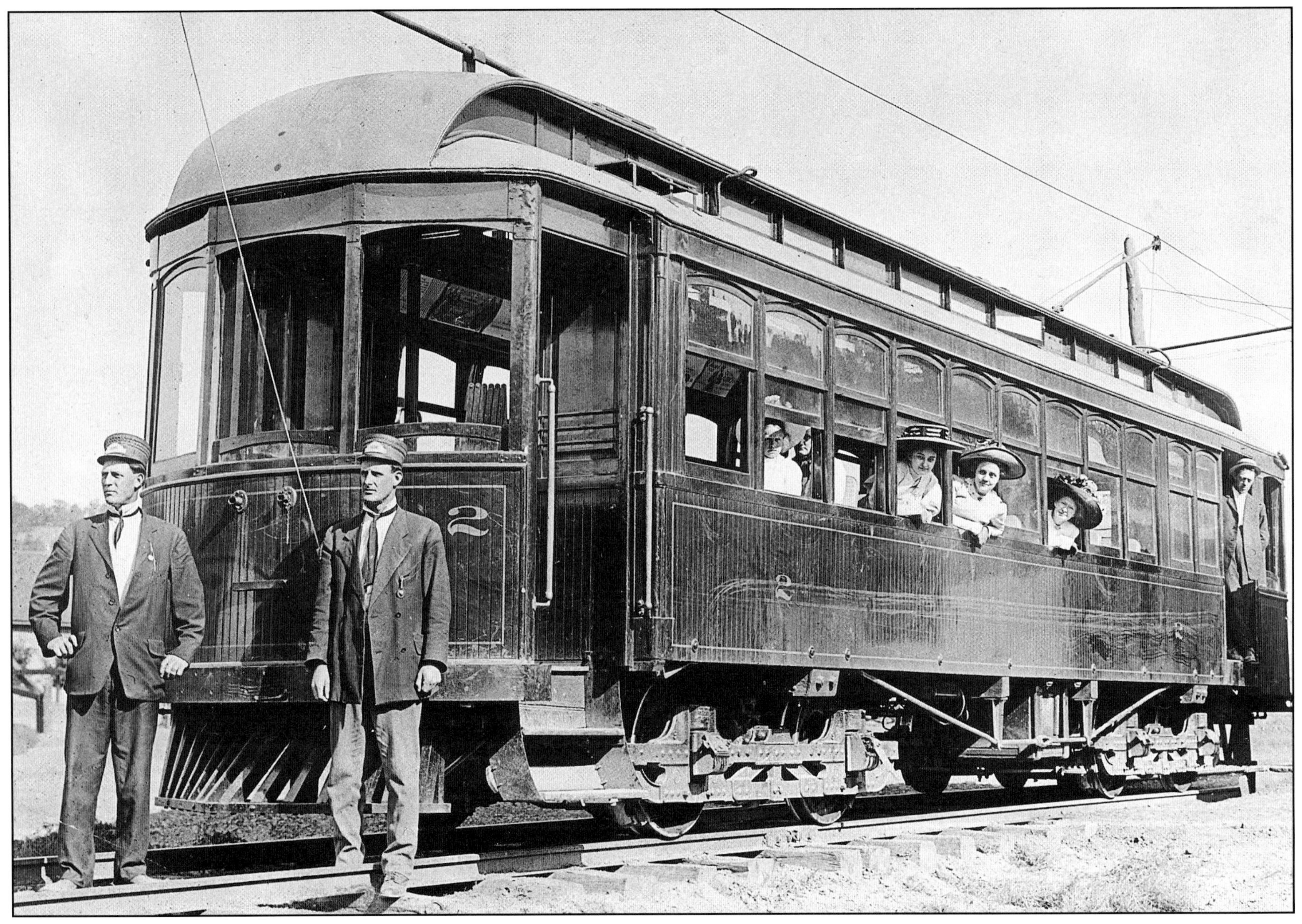

This photograph is a fitting one to conclude this brief look into the life and times of the streetcar in the Centennial State. Throughout the history of the trolley, whenever a camera was in evidence, most operators and private citizens alike were agreeable to having their pictures taken with the car. At the end of the line in Cokedale the crew of Trinidad Electric Transmission Railway & Gas Company 2 stands in front of the car as smiling, bonnet-bedecked young ladies lean out of the windows, and a gentleman passenger stands in the baggage doorway. Life may not have been any less complicated then than it is today, but folks seemed to enjoy it more. *([Interurban] Railroad Car No. 2, crew in foreground and passengers leaning out of windows, photographer unknown, no date, Mazzulla collection, Amon Carter Museum, Fort Worth, Texas)*

PAPER TIGERS

As with many ideas man dreams up, some become reality and others "die on the vine." So it was in the street railway era. Colorado was not unique during the fledgling years of the industry, for throughout the country the somewhat reckless promotions of the period led to the construction of many lines that should never have been built. Fortunately, some never made it off the drawing board as economics and leveler heads prevailed.

As we have seen, the City Railway in Leadville should never have employed an animal powered system, given the extreme climatic conditions under which it was expected to operate. That equation and the fact that it was under-financed spelled a quick death to the system in less than one year. In addition to its own financial problems, Aspen's horsecar line was also caught in the economic downturn of the early 1890s. The line only lasted about two years.

Industry publications reported in 1888 that the Canon City Street Railway Company had been formed with a capital of $30,000 to construct a horsecar line of three miles. Nothing came of it. And a street railway directory of 1891 listed the Cardiff & Glenwood Street Railway Company as intending to build a line in the Glenwood Springs area. As with the Canon City project, nothing was ever built.

Two known Colorado systems actually got off the drawing board, both surprisingly located in the same area. The Florence Street Railway generated enough financial support to survey a right-of-way between the town in its corporate name and Canon City. Equipment was actually ordered and built but never delivered, as the company exhausted its funds. The other project was more ambitious. It was to run between the above named towns and the Royal Gorge and was named Canon City Florence & Royal Gorge Railroad Company. A section of right-of-way was built, and there is speculation that equipment was ordered but never delivered, as this company also succumbed to under-financing.

The period of the 1880s and 1890s was a time of great expectation for those attempting to fund and build street railways. A great many of them turned out to be "paper tigers."

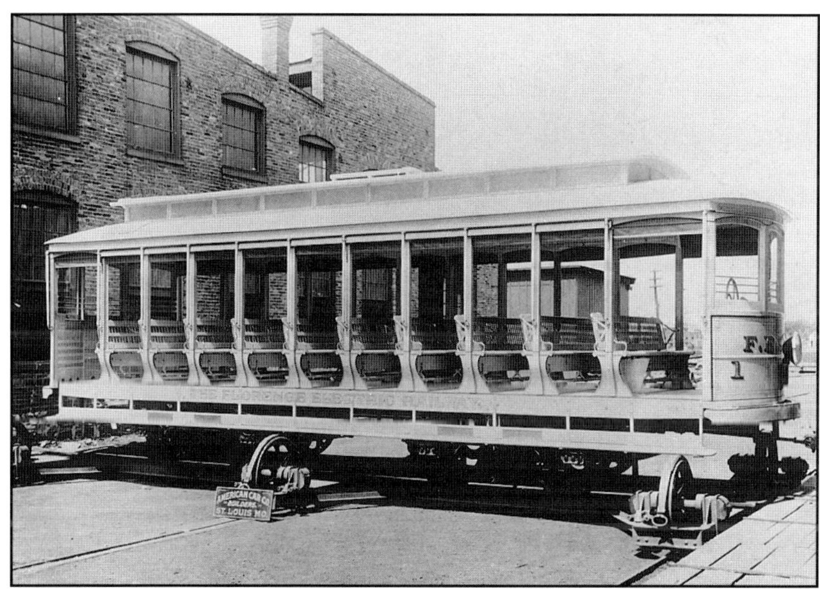

Open car 1 of the stillborn Florence Street Railway is pictured at the builder, American Car Company of St. Louis. This car and others that were built for the line were probably sold to an operating system elsewhere in the country. *(Don Robertson collection)*

BIBLIOGRAPHY

American Electric Railway Association, "Denver & South Platte Ry.," (Colorado), September 1926.

Blair, Edward, *Leadville: Colorado's Magic City*, Pruett Publishing Co., Boulder, Colorado, 1980.

Cafky, Morris and John A. Haney, *Pikes Peak Trolleys*, Century One Press, Colorado Springs, 1983.

Colorado, A Guide to the Highest State, Federal Writers' Project of Work Progress Administration, American Guide Series, Hastings House, New York, 1941; reprinted, University Press of Kansas, Lawrence, 1987.

Cox, Harold E., *The Birney Car*, published by the author, Forty Fort, Pennsylvania, 1966.

Sanford, Gladden C., "From Strolling to Streetcars," *Boulder Daily Camera*, FOCUS, January 21, 1979.

Helpland, Kenneth I., *Colorado Visions of an American Landscape*, Roberts Rinehart Publishers, Niwot, Colorado, 1991.

Hilton, George W. and John F. Due, *The Electric Interurban Railways in America*, Stanford University Press, Stanford, California, 1960.

"How a Small City Property Was Resuscitated," *Electric Railway Journal*, Vol. 71, No. 6, McGraw-Hill, New York, 1928.

Jones, William C. and Noel T. Holley, *The Kite Route, Story of the Denver & Interurban Railroad*, Pruett Publishing Co., Boulder, Colorado, 1986.

Jones, William C., Gene C. McKeever, F. Hol Wagner and Kenton Forrest, *Mile High Trolleys,* Pruett Press, Boulder, Colorado, 1975, 2nd edition.

McCoy, Dell and Russ Collman, *The Crystal River Pictorial,* Sundance Ltd., Denver, Colorado, 1972.

McGuire, William L. and Charles Teed, *The Fruit Belt Route*, Roder Graphics, Grand Junction, Colorado, 1981.

"Notes on the Grand Junction & Grand River Valley Railway," *Electric Railway Journal*, Vol. 36, No. 16, McGraw-Hill, New York, 1910.

"Office Building and Carhouse of Denver City Tramway Company," *Electric Railway Journal*, Vol. 37, No. 15, McGraw-Hill, New York, 1911.

"One-Man Cars for Greeley, Colorado," *Brill Magazine*, Philadelphia, March 1915.

"Operation to Cease in Trinidad," *Electric Railway Journal*, Vol. 62, No. 10, McGraw-Hill, New York, 1923.

"Order Entered to Dismantle Famous Colorado Line," *Electric Railway Journal*, Vol. 62, No. 22, McGraw-Hill, New York, 1923.

Osterwald, Doris B., *High Line to Leadville*, Western Guideways, Ltd., Lakewood, Colorado, 1991.

Ott, Richard, *When the River Was Grand*, Gazette Press, Grand Junction, Colorado, 1976.

Pearce, Sara J., *Guide to Historic Aspen and the Roaring Fork Valley*, Cordillera Press, Inc., Evergreen, Colorado, 1990.

Peyton, Ernest S. and Al Kilminster, "Last of the Birneys," *Colorado Rail Annual No. 17*, Colorado Railroad Museum, Golden, 1987.

Peyton, Ernest S. and R.A. Moorman, *Fort Collins Municipal Railway,* Pacific Railway Journal, Vol. 2, No. 2, San Marino, CA, June, 1957.

"Pueblo Cars Remodeled for One-Man Operation," *Electric Railway Journal*, Vol. 67, No. 23, McGraw-Hill, New York, NY, 1926

Reid, J. Juan, *Growing Up In Colorado Springs: The 1920's Remembered*, Century One Press, Colorado Springs, CO, 1981.

Smiley, Jerome C., *History of Denver,* Times-Sun Publishing, Denver, Colorado, 1901; reprinted, Unigraphic, Evansville, Indiana, 1971.

"Southern Colorado Power Converts to Buses," *ERA Headlights*, Electric Railroaders Association, New York, February 1948.

"Trinidad Electric Railroad Co.," *Street Railway Review*, Vol. 15, No. 5, McGraw-Hill, New York, 1904.

Vandenbusche, Duane and Rex Myers, *Marble, Colorado: City of Stone*, Golden Bell Press, Denver, Colorado, 1970.

Wilkins, Tivis E., *Short Line to Cripple Creek*, Colorado Rail Annual No. 16, Colorado Railroad Museum, 1983.